THE GIFT OF HOPE

Top Experts Share How Real People Changed Their Lives

THE GIFT OF HOPE

Top Experts Share How Real People Changed Their Lives

Linda Orr Easthouse & Brian L. Mathews

The Gift of Hope: Top Experts Share How Real People Changed Their Lives

Copyright © Linda Orr Easthouse and Brian L. Mathews. All rights reserved.

Published by The DP Group, LLC., PO Box 584, 150 Wrenn Drive, Cary, NC 27512, United States

ISBN: 978-1-949513-30-1

No part of this publication may be reproduced, stored in a retrieval system, or transmitted in any form or by any means, electronic, mechanical, photocopying, recording, scanning, or otherwise, except as permitted under Section 107 or 108 of the 1976 United States Copyright Act, without either the prior written permission of the publisher or author. Requests to the author for permission should be addressed to Linda Orr Easthouse and Brian L. Mathews or to the publisher at The DP Group, LLC., PO Box 584, 150 Wrenn Drive, Cary, NC 27512, United States.

Linda Orr Easthouse: Linda@naturalbioenergetics.ca

Director. Natural Bioenergetics Institute #115 1925 18 Ave NE Calgary, AB Canada T2E7T8

www.NaturalBioenergetics.ca

Brian L. Mathews Brian@NBGlobal.org

President, Natural Bioenergetics Global, a Corporation Number 1162954-9, incorporated under the *Canada Not-For-Profit Corporations Act*, PO Box 2541 Abbotsford Station A, Abbotsford B.C. Canada, V2T 6R3

www. NBGlobal.org

Printed in the United States of America.

First printing edition 2021.

Disclaimer

The authors and publisher have made every effort to ensure that the information in this book was correct at press time. However, the author and publisher do not assume any responsibility and disclaim any liability to any party for any loss, damage, or disruption caused by errors or omissions, whether such errors or omissions result from negligence, accident, or any other cause.

Adherence to all applicable laws and regulations, including international, federal, state, and local governing professional licensing, business practices, advertising, and all other aspects of doing business in the US, Canada, or any other country or any other jurisdiction is the sole responsibility of the reader and consumer.

Neither the author nor the publisher assumes any responsibility or liability whatsoever on behalf of the consumer or reader of this material. Any perceived slight of any individual or organization is purely unintentional.

The resources in this book are provided for informational purposes only. They should not be used to replace the specialized training and professional judgment of a health care or mental health care professional.

Neither the author nor the publisher can be held responsible for using the information provided within this book. Please always consult a trained professional before making any decision regarding treatment of yourself or others.

Each author's contact information is provided in her story. For information or questions related to authors' stories, please contact authors directly.

ADVANCE PRAISE FOR THE GIFT OF HOPE

Too often, we experience symptoms we don't understand, and we say to ourselves, "It just came out of nowhere, and it won't leave." But it came from somewhere down deep inside of us. It is like a flashing light warning of system overload. We need to slow down and take time to sort out our individual buried issues, often from our childhood. The practitioners in this book give helpful examples of the underlying causes as they listen to the body and follow up on the well-being of those who have been halted by burnout, breakdowns, traumas, and stress.

Natural Bioenergetics brings new hope to readers so that they can find clues to resolving mysterious symptoms that people have been stuck with for years.

Kathleen Condit
Biomagnetic Research, Inc.

For anyone considering embarking on a program of Natural Bioenergetics, this little book contains inspiring case studies illustrating what this therapy can accomplish.

Terry Larder
Founder and Director of the Classical Kinesiology Institute.
Author of "Essential Kinesiology Techniques for Muscle Testing Practitioners"

The Gift of Hope reveals gently through well-chosen real examples key aspects of NB's way and shows some of the wonders it can do. In this book, NB specialists share invaluable information about how some of their clients, some severely sick, having tried conventional and other therapies, gained health through personalized NB procedures. Specific examples of corrections are reported in parallel with people's symptoms, giving a taste of how trauma can be lifted, physiological illnesses transformed, and distress metamorphosed.

Through those cases, the reader is brought into a journey of discovery, receiving insights into the ways our intelligent bodies can go back to life, thanks to NB. While reading this book, one can feel how much NB empowers people because it helps them be who they are. And when that happens, they are grounded and strong, they are happy, and they shine! Not artificially, but naturally. They spontaneously live a healthier life, showing the way through their example. They lead and empower other people. After reading this book, you will probably sense that NB not only changes one person at a time in a truly amazing way but that it also transforms families and communities, giving them hope for a brighter future.

Thibaud d'Oultremont, Ph.D.
Research Project Director

The success stories that Ms. Easthouse and Mr. Mathews put together in this book shed a clear light on the wonderful healing potential of Natural Bioenergetics and will encourage those who suffer from physical ailments or mental distress to give it a try. They deserve our gratitude for undertaking this beautiful project, ultimately improving life quality for many people.

Rabbi Rephoel Szmerla, Lakewood NJ
Senior Rabbi

As an energy worker for over twenty years, I am deeply impressed with the fantastic results that are facilitated with Natural Bioenergetics. The stories are compelling and completely relatable. I am anxious to learn more about the process and find a practitioner for myself and my family.

Nancy Webster
Energy healer

NB'S MESSAGE

As with all great endeavors, some names readily leap to mind when one sits to think who is to be thanked for the existence of such a fine work. Such is the result of Natural Bioenergetics (Health Kinesiology) – a work deemed by its founder to cause "Miracles to happen every day; the impossible just takes a little longer." It is a work that for decades has changed the lives of many thousands upon ten thousands of people around the world in profound and wonderful ways. A mission that brings hope when all seems lost.

To whom do my gratitude and thanks go-to for this book that tells of the hope Natural Bioenergetics brings? First, to those whose names are considered "legendary" in the industry, those individuals who contributed untold amounts of time and energy in the development, practice, and perfection of the system called Natural Bioenergetics (HK). Had it not been for them, these stories could not have been written.

Then there are those who made this book project a reality. Linda Orr Easthouse and her tireless pursuit of seeing NB/HK promoted. Divya Parekh and her team at Dreams Accelerator went above and beyond in their support, guidance, and professionalism to see these stories told.

Last but not least are the practitioners and specialists who daily practice the discipline of NB/HK in their communities and who are simply considered "spectacular" by their clients. And of course, I thank the individuals in this book who were willing to tell of their experiences with NB/HK and share the gift of hope with those searching for freedom.

It is to these people that I dedicate this book. I am profoundly grateful to be included in their company. Together, may we continue to change the world for the better.

Brian L. Mathews
President, Natural Bioenergetics Global

CONTENTS

NB's Message	ix
Introduction	1
Permission to Succeed	5
Brian L. Mathews	5
The Oxygen Mask	17
Reili Hellmold	17
Finding the Piece of the Puzzle	25
Vivian Klein and Gillian Bauer	25
The Whole Rainbow: A Journey to Trust	37
Eva-Maria Willner	37
Lifting a Dark Cloud	45
Judy Friedman	45
Body, Mind, Spirit—and Heart	53
Cheryl Hannah Nicholson	53
Anxieties of a Vitamin Junkie	65
Franky Kossy	65
Peeling The Onion	73
Linda Orr Easthouse	73
Corrections for Allergy Suffering	81
David Schaffer	81
Hit From Behind	87
Mary Beth Skellorn	87
The Mind Does Not Like Pain	95
Brian L. Mathews	95
Removing the Fortress of Non-Protective Walls	105
Linda Orr Easthouse	105
From Hopeless to Hope and Happiness	113
Sharon Mathews	113
Successfully Self-Employed	123
Eva-Maria Willner	123
Animal Behavioral Issues	133

Cheryl Hannah	*133*
A New Lease on Life	139
Linda Orr Easthouse	*139*
A Natural Bioenergetics Primer™	147
Acknowledgments	155

INTRODUCTION

I was fighting burnout. My husband and I had just moved across continents, changed jobs, and struggled with two teens who faced physical and learning challenges while going through culture shock. From the metropolis of Lima, Peru to cowboy central in Calgary, Canada, it was too much for any of us. We were desperate for help. In addition, my new job entailed international travel, so I was away a lot, making the disaster on the home front worse.

As we struggled to get on our feet, I was introduced to a person who did a little Natural Bioenergetics (NB) work, although, back then, it was called Health Kinesiology (HK). He was just a student but did NB sessions with people just to help them. He was an angel in disguise for us. He gave us hope that there was a way through the disaster and that we could change years of health and learning, and emotional patterns.

It wasn't long until the miracles started happening. I was amazed at the changes that came from the sessions we did with him. I had to know what this stuff was. So I began the journey to learn it for myself. At the end of the first course, while waiting to fly home from California, I called my husband and told him, "I have found my calling. I have to do this full time." Then and there, I started the first steps on the adventure to become the best practitioner I could be. I had to share the hope I found through NB.

This book is a collection of stories from NB Specialists and Instructors worldwide sharing the stories of hope from their clients. Some of them even share their own story of hope. Each client's account is highly personal, and some share trauma or difficult situations. We changed the names of most clients in these stories (and some locations) to protect the families' privacy. As these stories sometimes include the description and naming of an aggressor, we respected the need for the complete privacy of our clients. Other than these specific pieces of information, these stories are 100 percent true ones.

If you are not aware of Natural Bioenergetics, it is a gentle, holistic therapy that addresses physical trauma and incorporates emotional, mental, and spiritual health. NB looks at the whole of life, providing an approach to personal development, health, and well-being.

As you will read in these real-life stories, NB uses "muscle monitoring" to access information from a person's subconscious mind so that the NB practitioner understands how to bring about health and well-being for a client. NB is based on interdisciplinary science. Specialists apply the science of mind-body-environment relationships.As well as integrating the wisdom of traditional eastern understanding of the body.

All of us wrote these stories to share the wonder and joy as we watched our clients transform their lives through NB. We want to share the profound power of this work with the world. We also wrote this book to support Natural Bioenergetics Global (NBG), a not-for-profit organization that provides the structure and rights to Natural Bioenergetics as a body of learning and techniques/technologies that make this all possible.

I appreciate your support in buying this book. All the profits from our stories go to NBG to promote this natural, energetic mode of life and health enhancement.

Mental and emotional well-being is a top issue these days. There is so much bad news, so it is a breath of fresh air to share these stories of transformation. So sit back, relax, and enjoy the book, knowing each tale has a real-life happy ending.

As you read this book, you will learn what can be achieved through Natural Bioenergetics. And you may begin to identify areas where NB would serve you in improving your well-being. I hope you get excited by the possibilities that await you through NB. As you meet the NB Specialists who share these stories of hope, I trust that you will reach out to them. They would be delighted to assist you on your journey.

Maybe after reading these stories, you can see yourself becoming a NB Specialist. It is an exciting, fulfilling career!

Reach out and chat with me or any of the specialists. We would love to help you explore if that is right for you.

As you relate with the transformation in each life in these stories, you will want to support that opportunity for others. NBGlobal is looking for partners, sponsors, and benefactors. Also, you likely will see others whom you know who are like the people in these stories, and you may want to give hope to people you know going through similar circumstances. Gifting this book, *The Gift of Hope*, is a gentle way to share hope.

Linda Orr Easthouse
NBG Volunteer Book Project Coordinator
Director Natural Bioenergetics Institute

Permission to Succeed

Brian L. Mathews

Bruce was CEO of a fast-growing software company, but his work performance suffered dramatically from migraines, and he was about to leave his job because of the severe, debilitating pain.

> *"I just kept getting severe migraines that lasted anywhere from 20-30 hours every couple of days. I was nauseous and experienced excruciating, inescapable, all-consuming pain. Here I had access to the best healthcare in North America, the best pharma had to offer but nothing worked. Even morphine did not help me." (Bruce)*

When I first discovered Natural Bioenergetics in 2009, I saw seemingly impossible events begin to occur. Debilitating, overwhelming pain and physical dysfunction simply began to go away. From the crippling effects of a ruptured disc to severe daily headaches resulting from a car accident to significant food allergies affecting a child's development, it seemed that miracles occurred. I had no idea what Natural Bioenergetics was, but I intended to find out. After attending the first course of NB training in 2010, I knew this was what I wanted to spend the rest of my life doing.

I share my client Bruce's story because it is a story after my own heart. As an entrepreneur is driven to build successful companies that push the limits of business dynamics, I had a clear understanding of why Bruce was so driven and the cost that passion can have on a person.

I heard of Bruce long before he came into my office. I worked with his wife and some of his children at different times over the previous 18 months. They expressed concern over Bruce's migraines and how he was affected by them. When he turned up in my office in November 2020, he was openly cynical about whether Natural Bioenergetics could help him. Bruce had suffered from migraines since he was 17 years old. He tried many traditional and non-traditional approaches to deal with the pain, which became debilitating because he was very concerned about his future.

Bruce was determined to have a significant impact on the world, and he was sidelined by pain. He was clearly a driven man who lived life at a very intense pace. I asked Bruce what finally brought him into my office:

"I'm the CEO of a publicly-traded software company in rapid growth mode. I missed key meetings and was not able to show up fully for work. My work performance suffered dramatically. I was going to have to leave my job because I was getting migraines so often. I worked with a neurologist for the last couple of years, and he had no more medications to give me and didn't know what else to do. My family doctor didn't know what to do either. I went through a bunch of other treatments, and I was desperate. My wife told me about you for a while, and I saw the success that she was having, so I decided to give Natural Bioenergetics a try."

Often, people come into our offices who have exhausted all other avenues and are willing to try something/anything to find relief from their complaints. Often the traditional resources find solutions for people's health and wellness issues; however, where is a person supposed to go when all available resources fail to resolve an issue? I am always careful to explain that we are not a medical resource. We do not treat, diagnose, or cure. We do not name a problem or focus on a single aspect of a person's health; that is an approach in medicine.

Natural Bioenergetics works with all the underlying energy systems of a person's biofield: the body, mind, and spirit. NB finds where energy is not flowing correctly and corrects the imbalance to restore proper energy function. Pain can be viewed as simply a misdirected energy signal indicating imbalances that need to be addressed. Energy is everything to the biofield.

As Bruce continued to share what he experienced, I gained a clearer picture of what was behind his misfiring energy system.

Bruce recounts:

"I just kept getting migraines, severe migraines which lasted anywhere from 20-30 hours, not necessarily every day but every couple of days. They bled into each other. I was down all the time, and these migraines were terrible, the terrible pain that medications did not solve. Even morphine did not help me. While the pain was throughout my body, it was centralized in my brain and bones.

I was nauseous. When I would experience that pain, all I could do was pace; I could not lie down, sleep or read. I could only pace for hours. I experienced excruciating, inescapable pain. It was all-consuming. Here I was with access to the best healthcare in North America, the best pharma had to offer, but nothing worked."

In the first session, we began to put some of the pieces of the energetic puzzle into place to bring about change, starting with a Bioenergy Control System: Alignment correction. This correction consists of four aspects: a body position/movement, a hand placement on the body, magnetism, and psychological thought.

This correction is specifically intended to realign how the biofield coordinates, utilizes and synchronizes the flow of energy found in these four aspects: the interface of physical movement, energetic flow through the meridian located in the hands, magnets, and their effect on the body's magnetic field, and the power of the mind. It is unusual to have this structure come up in a client's first session, as it is designed to realign the biofield after completing a significant amount of NB work.

I often see one of two dynamics occurring within their energy systems or biofield with clients new to Natural Bioenergetics. One dynamic is that they have low or little energy resources available. The initial NB work focuses on energizing the biofield so it has the resources for change. The second dynamic is that the client has significant energy resources available. The initial NB work focuses on restructuring and streamlining those resources for the proper function of the biofield.

Bruce fit in the latter category. It was clear his biofield had significant energetic resources; they just needed to be restructured and focused on growth rather than limitations. I often find this is the case with highly motivated and driven individuals. They have enormous capacity and just need assistance to lift to the next level of performance.

The second group was a Bioenergy Control System: Membrane Configuration:
— *Knowing I can get what I must get*
— *Knowing I can be what I need to be*
— *Knowing I must be able to do what I should.*

The third and last group of the session was a simple pair of Psychological: I feel/I am:
— *I feel drained*
— *I am needed.*

Bruce was back within six days for a second appointment. He experienced one day without pain, but other than that, he experienced 10 days of severe pain. We began the second session with another Bioenergy Control System: Alignment. His energy system was way out of alignment. Like a high-performance sports car, when the electrical system has melted wiring, blown fuses, and faulty programming, it will not function at the top end of its range.

Next followed a Symbiotic Energy Transformation (SET). This is NB's most powerful correction concerning updating the biofield's ability to recognize and address toxic load and introduce vibrational patterns for key functional elements within the body. The items within this group represented some of the various substances he was exposed to in the hopes that the products would bring about the relief he was looking for.

The last two groups of work began to open the door to what drove Bruce to push so hard in life. Both groups were Psychological:

Psychological: I feel/I am:
— *I feel unsuccessful*
— *I am sincere*
— *I feel disappointed*
— *I am bold.*

Psychological: Past, Present, Future:
— *Being broken in the Past*
— *Being disgusted in the Present*
— *Being nervous in the Future*

I next saw Bruce a month later, and he shared some exciting developments. He still experienced migraines, but things seemed different. A CEO can fuel drive and passion through "adrenal" energy, or that same drive and passion can be fueled by balanced and focused bioenergy. One can be very debilitating while the other is sustainable.

Bruce recalls how his stress response changed:

"After the second appointment, I started noticing how on a stressful day, I processed information differently. I seemed to be more neutral throughout my day. Work is very hectic; we deal with some of the most

valuable brands globally, the top names in the business. These are very demanding clients, and I noticed that when I had stressful days, it just didn't seem to affect me as much. I seemed to be a little bit calmer."

The third appointment consisted of only two groups of work. The first was a Bioenergy Flow Balance: Chakra correction. This correction addresses imbalances in the primary energy centers along the midline of the body. There are two aspects per item: a magnet and a thought:

— *South Seeking magnet over the Third Eye, think: "misjudged."*
— *South Seeking magnet over the Solar Plexus, think: "dissatisfied."*
— *North Seeking magnet over the Base Chakra, think: "demand."*

In the second group of work comes one of the highest levels of training: Psychological: Word Strings. The robust nature of this group is in the way it works with six different aspects of the biofield regarding three aspects of and within the body as well as three parts of the energy field that surrounds the physical body. Word Strings brings proper function to each group in and of itself and integrates all three with each of the other two—very complex work.

Psychological: Word Strings
— *Efficient, Scattered, Unreasonable, Immeasurable.*

Bruce was back within a week and reported that he had no migraines since the last appointment. During one particularly intense day at work, he had ten meetings and still no migraine. He was very encouraged by these results. When I asked him to reflect on what he was thinking during that fourth appointment, I had to laugh at his response:

"*What surprised me most was that it worked. I was stunned and shocked by that. I was very, very cynical about whether it was going to work. I was on heavy, heavy pharma medication, doing all sorts of other treatments at the time, so once I started eliminating my other treatments,*

I realized that NB was driving the changes in my improved health. I was shocked by how sudden it was.

I started having brilliant migraine-free days, and I could go to work — not only go to work but put in a long day. Previously, I was very reluctant to do a long day because I was worried that a migraine would come back. My job demands long days and requires attention. Now I was able to get through a long working day without having a migraine."

Bruce came into the office once a week for a month and continued to gain momentum. He experienced pain-free primarily days. The majority of the work in the NB sessions was psychological, dealing with insecurities, past trauma, poor choices, and self-doubt.

One of two breakthroughs for Bruce was his recognition that he lived in "fight or flight" mode his whole life. As he described it:

"When we began the process, I realized that I was always in fight mode; I was always tense. I've been in this mode my whole life. I'm an entrepreneur. I built two companies from scratch, and when you live that lifestyle, you tend to develop certain traits. One of the traits that I developed was to be ON all the time. My wife and I have six kids, so that's busy in and of itself. So I've always had a hectic, hectic life."

I could see Bruce approached Natural Bioenergetics in the same way he viewed life: at full throttle. However, his new awareness of being in "fight or flight" mode for most of his life expanded to include the second breakthrough: an understanding that he also sabotaged his effort to succeed.

Self-sabotage is something we all seem to have in common. It stops us from achieving the things we know we can do but never seem to pull off. We all have a "glass ceiling" that limits our growth and potential. In the limiting beliefs we planted in our subconscious, we are primarily rooted in fear and pain, meaning we only achieve what we believe we are allowed/able to achieve.

Bruce's newfound insight continued to unpack what held him back.

"My self-sabotage had to do with my first company. I did exceptionally well; we grew very fast and made a lot of money. We were on the front page of major newspapers; I was in magazines, we interacted at the highest level of society. We had a lot of success, and I started celebrating that success through partying. It got to the point where I drank too much, and had to quit. Once I got rid of those habits and the associated lifestyle, my life improved dramatically, but my business didn't improve right away.

I wanted the success that building a good company gives you—the personal gratification, the expanded influence, and the monetary benefit—but I didn't want the other things that came with my first success. I was afraid of going back to where I wasn't the best person I could be. I wasn't the best husband, father, or CEO of a company that I could be. When I look back in hindsight, I think that had a pretty significant impact on my health issues."

The session work Bruce did in the last two weeks spelled out what was going on in the deep recesses of his mind. It showed that he had a powerful sense and a fundamental determination to change the world around him. However, it also showed what held him back. The session started with a group of Body Brain Energy Integration (BBEI). These corrections remove interference fields and clarify energetic signals sent from the body to the brain. These interference fields develop very early in life, garble internal messages, and result in the brain sending incorrect commands back to the body.

Body Brain Energy Integration:
— *Fear of not being understood*
— *Fear that I am doubted*
— *Fear of not being worthy of respect*
— *Fear that I am insignificant.*

We also cleared some Psychological: Fears
— *Allowed to be what I want*
— *Blew it all up.*

This work was completed in the last appointment of the month under the title "Permission to succeed." Bruce's body gave an obvious picture of some of the triggers that kept Bruce sabotaging himself. By removing these stressors, the mind doesn't trigger "fight or flight;" instead, it stays focused on the tasks at hand, and there is profound clarity.
Psychological: Word Strings
— *Approval, Impact, Brilliant, Irresponsible.*
Psychological: Miscellaneous Concepts
— *Behavior*

While Bruce still has more work to do on his journey, he already has a significant positive impact on the world.
Bruce sums up the difference NB made in his life:

"I can't tell you how great a difference Natural Bioenergetics made in my life. First and foremost, for my family. The difference now makes me feel more secure for them. Now they don't see me pacing in pain. And then secondly, of course, my career. It's just unbelievable. I am more effective now than ever in my career. I approach things differently.

NB hugely impacted my success at work. Our company doubled in sales, and our stock price went up dramatically. I'm not saying that all of that is due to my NB work with Brian. But I am the CEO of that company; I have a significant impact on the company. The changes I experienced now allow me to have an even more significant impact in my company."

The essence of what Natural Bioenergetics did for Bruce was to utilize the power of his mind to identify and eliminate the stressors that triggered "fight or flight," which kept him from recognizing the fear and pain that held him back. Natural Bioenergetics gently peels away the layers of pain and trauma around these issues, enabling the mind to get close to them. Once the mind has safe access, it can process the pain, and suddenly clarity comes. It changes the direction energy flows and opens the mind to new information and opportunities.

Once we identified Bruce's stressors, removed the triggers, and shut down "fight or flight" mode, Bruce's mind was able to process significant bedrock issues and release that pain and fear, restoring the correct balanced flow of energy within his biofield. The rest of the process was the body just doing what it was made to do.

Are you an entrepreneur looking to blast through the glass ceiling? Natural Bioenergetics work helps you grow your business, your confidence, and your skills. It can help you stop the sabotage and make purposeful choices. Call me, and let's see if we are a good fit for what you need.

About the Author

Brian L. Mathews is an Advanced Natural Bioenergetics Specialist and has been working in the field of energy medicine and stress elimination since 2013. He is passionate about working with individuals trapped by harmful habits, limiting beliefs, and traumatic life experiences. Brian uses various disciplines and techniques designed to restore the body, mind, and spirit to optimal function. He has a strong reputation for supporting his clients in their journey towards freedom from the issues that stop them from becoming all they can be and living a life of joy and peace.

Brian is the President and Executive Director of Natural Bioenergetics Global, a Canadian Not-for-Profit organization that facilitates Natural Bioenergetic training worldwide. He is also Vice President of the NB Institute and sits on the NB International Council.

To schedule an appointment, email Brian@bioenergeticbydesign.com.
For information regarding Natural Bioenergetics Global and the 100-year vision, email: office@nbglobal.org.

The Oxygen Mask

Reili Hellmold

Elisabeth was diagnosed with burnout. She was tired, shaky, and crying a lot. It was clear she had been burning the candle at both ends. Elisabeth also had dramatic insomnia and extreme noise sensitivity—she even found the noise of cutting a cucumber too loud to bear!

> *"I no longer had the power to identify my needs." (Elisabeth)*

Having worked in an HR department for more than 15 years, the myths around the reasons for ending up in burnout were numerous. Especially working mothers like me tend to run into that crisis. When I decided to quit my job to dedicate all my energy to my husband and our three lovely kids, some of the managers came to my office with tears in their eyes telling me how lucky I was and what a stretch it meant to serve both worlds: Have a private life and be a business professional.

I was sincerely shocked as those managers had always pretended that everything was easy.

When I dropped out, it was clear that my central future

mission would be to coach and support working mothers and exhausted men and women.

It fills my heart with joy when my clients find authenticity, and I agree with Nelson Mandela in believing, "I am the master of my fate–I am the captain of my soul."

I'll never forget the phone call I received from my friend Elisabeth one lovely August morning. It was clear from her tone that this young working mother was having, or had a nervous breakdown. There was no glimpse of her characteristic energy and vitality whatsoever. Elisabeth told me that she had just been diagnosed with burnout and signed off work for the next couple of weeks.

From experience, I've learned that burnout is never a single-issue story. I find it usually occurs when both the private and the business side of life get out of balance. As long as one of these two sources of energy and happiness is stable, one can compensate or rebalance the other more easily.

There was no source left in Elisabeth's case that could nourish her soul in her everyday life. When she came to my practice for the first time, I immediately saw and felt the dire state in her nervous system. She was tired, shaky, and crying a lot. It was clear she burned the candle at both ends. She also had dramatic insomnia and extreme noise sensitivity—she even found the noise of cutting a cucumber too loud to bear!

Elisabeth's husband often worked out of town and was away from home most of the time. This left her with the responsibility of caring for their two children, then aged 5 and 7. Before this arrangement, the couple had already experienced a crisis in their marriage; so, their relationship increasingly became complicated.

She worked 20 hours per week in a very demanding role that also included travel. Elisabeth used to love her job; it was everything she had dreamed of. She put her heart and soul into all the projects and continued to fulfill what she thought was expected of her, to her now obvious detriment.

Our journey working together was like a treasure hunt of the utmost beauty. Finally, we disentangled the messed-up cords, and, with every knot that untied, Elisabeth became more resilient as her soul's glow began to emerge.

We started our work with energy corrections that would support her in retrieving inner peace. The first group was Psychological Imperatives; two commands that were paired with her primordial fear of losing control:

— *Stay true to yourself!*
— *You always have to adapt!*

Prior to our appointment, those imperatives gave her no choice but to feel and react to stress. The sentence, "Stay true to yourself!" was stressful because, on the one hand, this might have been what her soul shouted at her, but, on the other hand, she no longer knew how to stay true to herself. She lacked the power to identify her needs.

As she reflected on this statement, it became clear that there were times when she could not be 100 percent true to herself. However, Elisabeth also realized that staying true to herself was the only way she could lead an authentic life. It is also the only way for her to be a genuine mother. I was very touched when she realized that she created tremendous stress for her children whenever she was not true to herself. Children always feel whether their parents behave authentically or not.

When it came to adapting, Elisabeth gleaned a lot of insight about her childhood and how she grew up. Of course, all of us must learn to adapt to a certain extent, but Elisabeth realized that she would have to stop "adapting" if it violated her beliefs.

After that first rebalancing session, Elisabeth left my practice feeling energized and lighter. This was a good start for her journey back to energy and vitality. As we continued working together, we unveiled unhealthy belief systems and transformed them into empowering affirmations, which she repeated as homework. Step by step, her noise sensitivity diminished, and her nerves recovered.

For most of her life, Elisabeth had been a very self-aware and reflective woman who kept a regular diary, journaling and letting her emotions flow. However, when we started working together, I learned that she had not written anything for five years; she was simply too afraid of being overwhelmed by her emotions. After a couple of NB sessions, Elisabeth began writing a diary again.

As we moved on, we disentangled early childhood imprinting and reconstructed what led to her current situation. One important finding was how the role of a wife and working mother evolved and to what extent Elisabeth's position differs from her mother's.

Her parents' marriage resembled in some parts her own, but Elisabeth allowed herself to take a different path, her path, despite all obstacles and doubts. It was such a beautiful experience to feel the love that accompanied her during this process.

Elisabeth's love and appreciation for her parents and her childhood, alongside the partially painful insights, resembled a healing golden shimmer. This shimmer helped her heal her heart and her past. This shimmer radiated into her future as well.

We also made precious discoveries as we "identified" her inner self. When Elisabeth first came to my practice, she was quite a mess with no connection to her soul or inner voice.

She had a craving for self-efficacy and clarity, an urge to be back in the driver's seat of her life. Yet, at first, Elisabeth had neither the power nor the belief that this could happen. Then, one magic pair of Psychological Being / Not Being corrections did the trick. For Elisabeth, it was:

— *Being brave / Not being brave.*

Brave to end her relationship, brave to move forward, brave to communicate her needs and thoughts in her job, brave to stand up for herself!

When we do Being / Not Being corrections, we realize a dichotomy—a "damned if you do, damned if you don't" type of situation. For Elisabeth, this correction was one more important step towards authenticity; she now had the choice to be brave or not, depending on the situation. Without the stress around bravery, she became empowered to retake responsibility for herself.

The more often she came to see me, the less nervous she became. Slowly but surely, Elisabeth retrieved her inner wisdom and power. She allowed herself to take the chance to go on a retreat, cherishing the time with herself and others who were in a similar situation. She returned nourished with new energy and clarity.

A couple of weeks later, we dove into a psychological group focused on abundance:
— *Being abundant and following my own path*
— *Following my own path and being abundant*
— *Following my own path and being strong*
— *Being strong and abundant*
— *Being abundant and feeling happiness.*

Writing down these items gave me a shiver. They outlined so beautifully Elisabeth's path to happiness and how everything is related. These items invite us to take a deeper look and expand our comfort zone. It fits my life motto: Everything will fall into place.

Do you remember Tetris, the game where you have to get all the pieces to fit together? For me, life is like that game: God sends us challenges of all kinds, shapes, and sizes. Often, we don't know what the challenges are to teach us. But if we remain patient, reflective, and take a good look at the challenges, eventually, we will come to understand their message—or sometimes just let go!

For Elisabeth, NB was the key to reconnecting with herself, the key to sorting out her inner Tetris. With every session, Elisabeth regained her power to disconnect from unhealthy energies. She filled her heart and soul with self-love and followed her path to self-care and self-efficacy. Elisabeth could see the snares in her life and cut or avoid them. She felt relieved and secure as the old patterns dissolved. This created space for the "new Elisabeth" to emerge.

She realized that a healthy life with children follows one of the most critical rules during flight turbulence: make sure you place the oxygen mask over your mouth and nose first before you help your children. This beautiful analogy expands to all situations in which your help is needed; as long as you have enough oxygen yourself, you will be able to assist others.

In Elisabeth's case, this meant she had to make sure that she had enough "oxygen" by starting to meditate again and follow her heart and soul path to new fields of inspiration and spirituality. All those beautiful paths nourish her like roots nourish a healthy tree.

Our journey working together was like a treasure hunt of the utmost beauty; we disentangled the messed-up cords, and with every knot that untied, she became more resilient as her soul's glow began to emerge.

Today, Elisabeth lives an essentially healthy, and appreciative life. She is able to steer a clear-cut course in her work life, keeping a solid energy level.

Whenever I meet Elisabeth now, I am filled with humbleness and gratitude for having had the opportunity to accompany her on her journey. I am still touched and honored that she allowed me to work with her and watch her get back her glow.

About the Author

Reili Hellmold works as an NB practitioner, speaker, interpreter, and coach for authenticity, happiness, and inspiration to accompany her clients on their paths to their beaming selves.

One of her core questions is always: Who, if not you?

She loves her work with women who want to overcome any sort of crisis or strive for authenticity.

Accompanying older people during similar processes or those in grief asks for her unique empathy and coaching children through the rough waters of puberty or the school system. Yet, to see them start growing and blooming again in their very own radiance gives her all the motivation she needs.

Contact Reili to begin your journey to a happy, authentic life. Contact Reili:
www.reilihellmold.de
Email: hallo@reilihellmold.de

Finding the Piece of the Puzzle

Vivian Klein and Gillian Bauer

Gillian had debilitating migraines, in addition to enduring peri-menopause, which prevented her from working and even performing the most basic of tasks.

> *"I had labeled myself as someone that had migraines, and that's how it would always be. After the NB session, I no longer felt a victim or a sufferer, and I felt free of migraines. NB served me not just as a therapy for well-being, but also as a learning tool for life." (Gill)*

I am Vivian Klein, a Natural Bioenergetics Specialist. Since the outbreak of the COVID-19 pandemic, I now work with clients online through Zoom. Gillian (Gill) Bauer also is an NB specialist, and we met on Zoom during an update course for advanced NB. Afterward, as you'll see when reading this story, we worked together on eliminating her migraines, with Gill as the client.

Natural Bioenergetics is the most comprehensive system I have come across in my vast experience with complementary therapies. It allows practitioners to include and use everything they know. Before I experienced NB, I tried many therapies, including homeopathy, Alexander Technique, reflexology, nutrition, and others. No other system managed to touch upon my whole being like NB. My profound wish has always been to assist my fellow humans with the ability to facilitate and cause true healing in the most natural way possible.

I have facilitated many healing miracles over the years; yet, I don't consider myself a healer. Your body is its healer, with its brilliant healing mechanisms. Each person has an innate ability to stay well or to be coaxed back to wellness with the correct information and tools at the right time. My job as a practitioner is to facilitate change in the best, most efficient, and beneficial way possible. The knowledge I have acquired over the last 30 years is what I use as I work, all the while remaining the neutral "casual observer of what is" to enable healing in clients. My best work is like a finely crafted puzzle that challenges me to get every piece in the right place, in the proper order, at the right time.

With NB, sometimes the changes are slow and steady, taking months to realize a shift. Sometimes there are small miracles in every session. And, sometimes, there are authentic "aha" moments that are always so satisfying for everyone concerned. The experience I had with Gill demonstrates one of these aha moments.

Gill recalls when we met and how that led to healing her of migraines:

"When I was first introduced to Vivian, a fellow NB Specialist, I realized it was a perfect opportunity to work with an experienced and highly skilled NB teacher. I jumped at the chance and knew precisely what ailment I needed support with: Migraines.

As an NB Specialist, it's not always easy or appropriate to work on oneself. The ability to self-test using muscle monitoring for day-to-day issues is a fabulous tool and a skill for life. Sometimes, when we try to deal with our problems, we must work with our own unconscious biases and beliefs systems. There may be aspects that are hidden from our awareness, so it's always best to seek the skill set of another practitioner.

In the NB community, we work together to support each other in our roles, promote self-growth, self-development, and keep our energy vibrant and robust. Energetically and emotionally, NB Specialists continue to work on themselves to be the best practitioners they can be. We have our issues, trauma, and past to overcome. Being an NB specialist does not make us exempt from life's stressors; instead, it helps us overcome them and live to our fullest potential. Whatever we seek for others, we also strive for ourselves."

I wholeheartedly agree with Gill. Specialists are sometimes blind to what or how things happen to us and what we need to allow, correct, or change in ourselves. On the other side of the coin, we are sometimes hypersensitive and have good self-awareness, which does not necessarily mean that we are the best person to work on ourselves.

Gill explained in that first meeting the physical and emotional challenges she had because of migraines. She said migraines had plagued her for over nine years, with the symptoms steadily becoming worse.

Gill explains how the migraines affected her:

"Migraines are debilitating. A migraine will stop you in your tracks, prevent you from working, and stop you from performing even the most basic tasks like driving. You become ultra-sensitive to sounds and smells, and the most you can do is go to a dark, quiet room.

The migraines affected me most in the middle of the night. Like an alarm clock, the pain would wake me at around 2:00 a.m. and cause me to suffer with an upset stomach, vomiting, or both, so much so that I would be up and down to the toilet for the remainder of the night. Without sleep, I was left feeling bruised and wholly exhausted the following day. Migraine didn't just last a few hours; I felt the side effects for 24-48 hours.

My migraines seemed to start from nowhere. But, in hindsight, there were clear triggers, the main trigger being the effects of my going through peri-menopause. It appeared that my hormones and migraines followed a similar pattern; like clockwork, I would get a migraine the day before my period began. But, like most women, I just put up with it; it became part and parcel of the hormonal and menstrual cycle.

But as I traveled through the peri-menopausal journey, my menstrual cycles became even more erratic. I no longer bled every 28 days; instead, I had two bleeds per month and two migraines to go with it! I did what most do and sought the guidance of my local general medical practitioner. Unfortunately, he was not very supportive and prescribed three solid migraine tablets that made me feel anxious and made me vomit even more than the migraine itself."

Journaling is an excellent way for people to track their symptoms and occurrences. Gill started journaling and studying her migraines, looking for patterns, and trying to eliminate any triggers to ascertain what type of migraines impacted her. I asked her to share what she discovered through her journaling.

"I seemed to be sensitive to external environments such as a change in weather; high barometric pressure triggered a migraine. Dehydration and exertion from certain exercises, sports, or movements would bring on muscle tension in my neck and shoulder, which would then instigate a migraine. Clearly, the migraines were vascular, as they would occur the day before menstruation. The only holistic armor that worked for me was ice, rest, and meditation."

Gill also shared what she felt was the worst aspect of the migraines in its effect on her life.

"It was the uncertainty of when a migraine would strike next. When you work and haven't slept the night before due to a migraine, having to perform a full day in the office, or teach, look after children and family, can be a real struggle. Unless you've experienced one, you can't understand how migraine can knock the stuffing out of you.

In the end, you just get on with it, do your best. The kids and those around me just got used to my taking myself off to bed, saying, "Mum's got one of her headaches again!" Luckily, I am self-employed, so, to some extent, I could juggle my schedule. But can you imagine working in corporate life, trying to hold down a job with timelines, meetings, and programs while debilitated with migraines?"

When we began sessions to work on her migraines, Gill recalls that she went to the first appointment with curiosity and an open mind, hoping to receive help, however minor. She says she realized that "any relief would be an enormous benefit to the quality of my life." She says she was pleasantly surprised by the result of that first session.

Our first session together was wonderfully simple and basic. We did three groups of energy corrections. We started with a Belief System Elimination, eliminating the stress around a belief, which in turn pretty much makes that belief a non-issue, whether it was conscious or not.

— *Life can be flawed.*

Following that came two more sets of corrections that also worked in Gill's BioEnergetic Control System. These worked at the cellular level in the body's inner workings, which included hormone (re-)balance.

We then reset the spin of energy at major energy points internally and on the surface of Gill's body so that the energy could spin in the correct direction for her body.

Gill recalls the results of that first session:

"I went the most prolonged period of time without a migraine after just one appointment—eight amazing weeks. I hadn't been free of a migraine for that long in nine years. As an NB Specialist I witness how amazing NB can be for clients. So, I did not doubt that I would benefit from our session in some energetic way, but I was surprised at the extent our session had on me.

The very first protocol that came up in the session, "life can be flawed," was something I couldn't relate to at first. I could strongly feel how resistant I was to it. After the session, I sensed that, before the session, I must have had some sort of belief that "I was a migraine sufferer." But after the session, that belief no longer seemed to be there. I had labeled myself as someone that had migraines, and that's how it would always be. After the session, I realized that belief had diminished; I no longer felt a victim or a sufferer; I felt free of migraines."

I have seen Belief System Eliminations work like this over the years. People often remark that they could not relate to the sentence or sentences (beliefs) that came up because they were buried deep in the subconscious. The body brings them up energetically to be dealt with at the right time. It allows us to become conscious or aware of beliefs and behaviors that are no longer of use.

Recently, I asked Gill how the changes from our working together impacted her life. She exclaimed, "I feel free!"

Gill shares details about the impacts in her life from NB sessions:

"My life has returned to some sort of normality. I clearly noticed the reduction of tension and stress around a situation that may prompt a migraine. For example, travel abroad requires an early start, reduced sleep, excitement, missed meals, dehydration, and uncomfortable seating positions on the plane. Any one of those conditions in the past was enough to trigger a migraine. When I had the opportunity to put air travel to the test, none of these factors seemed to be problems; they didn't even enter my conscious or unconscious mind.

Multiple aspects of my life changed without our directly or specifically tackling them in our session. We did not work on how getting up early to go to the airport may be stressful; it just ceased to exist, unconsciously. At the time, I wasn't able to put two and two together; but with hindsight and reflection, it is evident that many things changed for the better.

Another positive aspect that I learned through this experience is that I realized many other women suffer too. My journey with migraines gave me a better understanding of what women have to deal with, how emotionally, mentally, and physically draining this condition is. In addition, I realized how unsupportive and lacking in understanding the medical profession, in general, is about menopause, which in turn set me on my path to becoming a Women's Health Specialist and Menopause Coach."

Gill also learned a lot about herself in the process. She explains how that came about:

"I thought I knew myself. I am an empathetic and very consciously aware person. But perhaps I don't know all the deep parts of myself, especially the aspects that may have been hidden, that were acting to impede or prevent me from living my full potential. Do we ever really get to see the deepest, darkest corners of our core?

During the many training courses we are required to complete to become NB Specialists, we become the client as well as student. We get on the couch to experience the energy pattern for ourselves and sense what the client may encounter, and, of course, we benefit personally from the protocols. This all helps us know ourselves better, tackle difficult life experiences in a safe and supportive environment, and be compassionate with fellow students and our clients. So, ultimately, we become better practitioners. It was good to be a student again!"

I recently asked Gill if she was surprised that the positive results happened so quickly and that she went so long after the initial session without a migraine. She responded that she was surprised and then further explained her reaction.

"After those eight weeks free of migraines, in the middle of the night, I awoke with pain over my right eye that usually indicated I was fighting off an infection. I had been bitten several times by mosquitoes the day before and had a nasty reaction to them. At first, I was fearful, "Oh no,

the work Vivian did hasn't lasted. "But there was a different feel to this type of migraine; the insect bite infection drove it. Still, this showed me how fearful I was of getting another migraine and that I believed that the migraines might return. So, I arranged a second appointment to tackle this new development.

This made me start to go deeper into what was really behind those nasty migraines. What came up was a deeper understanding of how my behavior may contribute to the problem.

I am passionate about what I do, about NB, and looking at different ways of working with my clients.

I like to set targets and goals to achieve. Appropriately in the second appointment, a focus on 'being addicted to goals' seemed to fit well. As a result, I started to give myself more time off, be less demanding, and stop placing unnecessary pressure on myself to do things."

Gill did so much work on her migraines over the prior nine years before we met that it only took a minimal amount of work to lay them to rest finally. I find some people need to analyze and dissect every single "disease" they have. In therapy, sometimes one might suddenly understand what they want, need, feel, etc. But sometimes understanding is the booby prize. What do we do with the understanding? How do we process it?

With NB muscle monitoring response, we can take the guesswork out of any condition, symptom, illness, or issue that the client brings to us. We work from the inside out; we observe what is—not what we think that person needs. The body has the answers. We learn to put our own stuff aside and use the NB framework and protocols, in addition to whatever other skills we may have, to offer the client's energy system what it needs and only do the work at the specific time the body is ready for it and can process it.

Sometimes we test, and something comes up through the

muscle monitoring that a client had not previously shared. Usually, the client says incredulously, "How did you know that?" I didn't; the body told me.

My firm belief is that NB is easy! This is one of the basic rules of NB: We need not always know exactly what is going on for a client to help them attain a better level of wellness. Any information the client gives us is usually helpful but not always necessary. Using accurate and careful muscle monitoring, we can access any information from the energy body that we need. With clarity of concept and thoughtful muscle monitoring, we can find the exact pieces of the puzzle, eliminate unnecessary guesswork, and short-cut the process to exactly whatever is most efficient and beneficial for a client at any given time.

Gill shares her final verdict about the work we did together:

"Awareness was key. It wasn't about stopping certain behaviors as such; it was more a realization of fears about moving my body, that a storm would trigger a migraine, concerns around blood sugar fluctuations, etc. I realized I gave my migraines a label, power, permission to be there. To an extent, my firm belief that I suffered from migraines gave it capital-M status. I hadn't realized I did that.

I no longer consider myself a sufferer of migraines! I think that was the most powerful thing that I took from our experience."

Gill shares more about the difference this work made for her:

"It gave me back my confidence, faith, and enjoyment of life. Going through menopause is a transition in itself and has many symptoms. The migraine aspect made this transition so much more difficult. It was as if I had become stuck, trying to hold back the tide, holding onto certain patterns of being, and not allowing myself to go with the flow or move with grace, courage, and calm through the storm that was the menopausal journey.

I now feel that, just like waves in a stormy ocean, my attitude towards menopause is more fluid and calm. This was an amazing learning curve that will only further my becoming a better NB Specialist and Menopausal Coach."

Finally, in a recent conversation with me, Gill shared her opinion of the outcome of her journey:

"Not only have I witnessed and experienced the amazing benefits of NB as a Specialist, observing how my clients' lives improve, but I've also experienced how profound and life-changing NB has been in my own life. NB came into my life through synchronicity at a time when I needed it most. It served me not just as a therapy for well-being but also as a learning tool for life."

About the Author

From the worlds of both art and business, Vivian started her NB career 30 years ago and has been a Natural Bioenergetics™ Specialist (previously HK—Health Kinesiology™) since 1991, having completed her extensive training in England (a rigorous training that included studies in Anatomy and Physiology, Counseling Skills, Nutrition and Practices Management/Business skills). Vivian was certified as an NB/HK /Instructor in 1995 by Jimmy Scott, Ph.D., the originator of Health Kinesiology/Natural Bioenergetics. She currently lives and practices in northern California. Vivian serves on the Natural Bioenergetics International Council.

Gillian is the facilitator of Health, Fitness & Kinesiology from Essex, UK using a comprehensive and empowering approach to uniting you with your whole self. She incorporates health of the body, mind, and spirit, integrating all her qualifications and modalities and over 12 years working with clients as a Natural Bioenergetics (Health Kinesiology) Practitioner. She is currently in the process of creating a unique program for Women called MENOCIZE.

Contact Vivian:
Email: evivi@sonic.net
Website: Viviklein.com
Phone: 707 538 8679
Text: 707 695 0719

Contact Gillian:
Email : gill.bauer@btinternet.com
FB: Health, Fitness & Kinesiology
FB: Sail thru (Peri to Post) Menopause
Website www.Tranquil-waves-of-motion.co.uk

The Whole Rainbow: A Journey to Trust

Eva-Maria Willner

Because of her parents, Jana grew up believing that relationships are based on drama and inherently unsafe. Drama, jealousy, battles, shouting, and crying were the only atmosphere she experienced while growing up. Her goal was to feel alive and to be part of something meaningful, and have meaningful relationships.

> "My parents instilled in me the attitude that either life is 'good' (so, don't bring up issues), or it is 'totally bad' (so, be ready to escape). My father always had his suitcase packed. As a kid, I hated my father for his behavior. But I learned that same behavior from him." (Jana)

Jana came to me because she heard about me from a friend of mine. She heard that I traveled a lot. I worked in other countries on various projects. My husband and I own a seminar house where people from many continents visit and study kinesiology or attend meditation retreats or dance therapy weekends.

Jana felt she could trust me because I could understand her need to travel the world and bring different sides of me together in the outer world. This was the key for her to come to me and trust me in the Natural Bioenergetics coaching sessions. Another key for her was that I am a woman.

I understood her well because I could never go to a therapist or a coach who never looks out of the box, does not see different countries or lifestyles, and does not try various methods. The technique is only half of the cake; my life experiences are equally important.

I hitch-hiked through Europe from ages 18 to 23. I worked in Israel in a kibbutz. I meditated in India in an Ashram and enjoyed being in silence in a monastery. I lived in community growing gardens, sharing cars, and many environments needed to create a sustainable world. I did tandem jumps in paragliding and skydiving (experiences that I am glad I did in a time where I could still do them). At a certain age, one looks back and thinks: why didn't I do it then?

So, clients who come to me know that I can support them in their "hunger for life" and their need to feel nourished and have meaningful experiences that stretch them. Life is not about consuming and being entertained; it is about getting creative and more intuitive and about what feels right in a moment with all the circumstances around. It's about bringing together the longing for spiritual growth and having fun and responsibility as a world citizen.

Jana had this hunger for life, but she doubted she could achieve meaningful experiences and relationships.

She describes how she felt before her first NB session with me:

"I felt empty, even though others saw me as an adventurous gypsy girl. Inside, I felt being a gypsy didn't fit anymore. I played the role of feeling safe. Being unattached and traveling helped me get through some rough years, and maybe it was appropriate in my late teens and twenties. Now, I felt I would end up a very bitter, old woman if I didn't change.

But I had no idea how to change or who I wanted to be. A friend told me about Bioenergetic Wellness, especially about NB and what it did for her in sessions. So, I dared to make my first appointment with you."

Jana is an only child, a loner, and never felt part of a group. As a child, when she came home from school, she never knew if her father's suitcase or her mother would be waiting outside the apartment door. She lived with the constant threat that her father would move out, and he blackmailed her mother that he would leave.

Jana grew up believing that relationships are based on drama and inherently unsafe. Her parents never separated, but the theme permeated her life from the beginning. This atmosphere of drama, jealousy, battles, shouting and crying was the only atmosphere she experienced.

This, of course, shaped her trust or mistrust in relationships, in men, and in life in general. She had no siblings or other family to share her doubts, fears, anger, insecurity, and shame. She was left alone to face it all. Jana felt profoundly helpless facing these experiences and ashamed to share them with friends. She handled all alone. She started to close down more and more.

She saw the tears and breakdowns of her mother. Over and over, she saw the infidelity of her father, but he never left. She watched as her mother just put up with it, year after year.

In one NB session, she had the insight that she copied the behavior of her mother in her childhood. But in her teens, she took her father's role: wanting to be free, not taking responsibility, not saying where she was going.

During her teens, she rebelled strongly. She tried drugs. She always felt like an outsider. Looking back now, she feels she was lucky not to have landed in the gutter.

Jana knew she needed to be vital to survive. So, she got strong and drove a motorbike, traveling the world. She learned to connect with people on an easygoing, superficial level. She worked on big cruise ships as a hairdresser and enjoyed meeting people from all around the world.

But she felt over the years that all this connecting felt more and more superficial. The "easy-living holiday feeling" was OK in her twenties. Jana enjoyed those years, but the alcohol or other drugs every night with the other crew members began to get old. Deep inside, she felt she did not want to go on like that.

By the time she came to me, she had experienced a lot but never had a long-term relationship. She longed for real affiliation, a deep connection that she had never experienced. The relationships she had were always fun and easy going like still being a teenager. Jana liked the "easy rider" feeling when she drove her motorbike, but she knew it was no longer appropriate in her mid-thirties. She longed for more.

After just one session, Jana found the courage to move out of her horrible cellar apartment, which was just the place from where she traveled to somewhere else. It was home base but not home. She found an apartment that had a lot of daylight and began to create a home.

Her goal was to feel alive. She wanted to be part of something meaningful, have meaningful connections and relationships, and not just swing between playing the macho-independent or the "needy little girl" who can't trust anyone, let alone trust a man.

Jana describes how she felt in that session:

"I always reflected on my life, but from the head, I just couldn't change anything. The NB sessions always surprised me. Insights came like a wave, also my tears and sobbing, and then the pain ebbed. There was suddenly this knowing. Me, my body, my cells let go of something, and I felt different. It was like my cells were reprogrammed. Old pain just melted away. I was surprised by myself that I could open up so much in the sessions and understand what you explained to me. I felt safe with you."

As we continued to work, she found new friends and a good network. Now, she likes her work and no longer feels the need to always be on the road or keep herself always super busy. As she says, "I am still a work in progress like we all are."

Using NB, we tested the priorities and, over six months, de-stressed and integrated many of the emotions driving her behavior. We balanced the major concepts doing just a few of the following each session:
- trust
- being trustful - not being trustful
- being associated - not being associated
- bonding
- men
- relationships
- her father
- her mother
- the parents together
- being in control - not being in control
- being open - not being open
- being vulnerable - not being vulnerable
- being alone - not being alone
- being disappointed - not being disappointed.

In the sessions, her body chose a lot of the NB balances around "being—not being." This procedure deals with polarities in life, learning to accept duality. For Jana, much of it was being able to set boundaries, have feelings, and the inner knowledge of when is it appropriate to be in control and when is it fair to not be in control.

She describes her journey:

"I really feel I have been on a journey of trust to trust myself, my intuition, my female side. And also other people. When new issues come up, I always book another session with you. The journey as a human being is so much easier with the support of sessions."

Jana cried a lot during the sessions. It felt like her stress, her disappointments, could melt away. She recognized the blows with herself. She had to forgive herself. She could see her self-pity and began to overcome it.

Jana explains more about her journey:

"I felt I had to take my armor down, which I was the most afraid of, but I thought I had to do it. It felt that a phase of my life was over and that I would end up a very hard, old, frustrated woman if I didn't.

I felt it was time to open up for something new. I felt safe with you and the procedures from NB. You explained to me that the items could only come up when I can deal with it. Only what I can handle and process and integrate will show up at a particular time."

In just one year, she made new friends. She describes how she felt about this: "We can journey together in life." For the first time in her life, she could feel like a member of a group where she felt bonded. Suddenly, she found "fellow travelers" on her path.

In the past, her few male relationships were long-distance relationships; so, she didn't get too close, and she could always leave by flying "home."

She started to develop new experiences with men. They no longer needed to be from another country where the long-distance relationship kept the man exciting but prevented a long-term relationship. She says, "NB allowed me to have a close relationship with a man for a few years."

Jana's parents' attitude towards her was that she was unreliable and could not be responsible. They only saw her as traveling, changing jobs often, and unable to have a relationship.

Jana describes how she grew up:

"I learned that I grew up seeing the world as black or white. Now, I also see shades from white, gray, to black. This black-or-white pattern came from my parents, who instilled in me the attitude that either life was "good" (so, don't bring up issues), or it was "terrible" (so, be ready to leave, to escape). I finally understood why my father always had his suitcase packed. I learned how much, as a kid, I hated my father for his behavior

and that I realized that same behavior from him. I played that game for so many years.

Nowadays, I can be the "whole rainbow." I can be open and closed. I can be with someone together and also be alone. I am not afraid anymore of transition times. In the sessions, I learned a lot about life itself."

Today, Jana is a single Mom. She has clear boundaries and handles her role very well. She has solid friendships and a sound support system around herself.

Here is how Jana describes her life now:

"I am more open, even more, bubbly than before, when I want to be. But I also can be quiet and enjoy myself alone. I am different with other people, and I can approach men differently. I trust myself now."

Working with Jana reminds me how important it is to examine oneself and grow continually. Think about yourself: Which outdated views or patterns from your parents and your upbringing in the family are still running your life? Would it be better to let some of that fade away?

I learn with every client and session to stay alert, to examine what serves me in my life and purpose and what no longer serves me. Many times, our parents didn't have choices. But we do. What do you want to change in your life?

About the Author

For over 30 years, Eva-Maria Willner worked with various kinesiology directions, coaching techniques, movement, and meditation. Whether it is individual sessions, groups, team coaching, or training, her focus is supporting people to be more aware of themselves, tune in to their inner guidance, and find their path. She is convinced that everyone has a purpose and that NB provides techniques to hear "your inner call" so that you have the courage and energy to go for it. In recent years, one of her focuses is aging well, staying inspired, fulfilled, and healthy.

She is the Founder and leader of the Meridianum Kinesiology Institut since 1998 in Germany, NB-teacher and teacher trainer, Transformations Kinesiology educator, Meditation teacher, Dance therapist, and Coach. She also is Co-Owner of a delightful Seminarhaus in the Black Forest (Schenkenzell, Southern Germany), where the year-round classes, workshops, and training happen.

Eva-Maria Willner
Meridianum - Institut und Schule für Kinesiologie
Reinerzaustrasse 24
D-77773 Schenkenzell
Germany
Telephone: 0049 (0)7836 - 957 9922
Fax: (0049) (0)7836 - 957 9911
Email: emw@meridianum.de
Website: www.meridianum.de
www.facebook.com/Meridianum-Institut-und-Schule-für-Kinesiologie

Lifting a Dark Cloud

Judy Friedman

Rachel had a tormenting rash for over three years. Despite more than five decades of therapy, 18 months of journaling, seeing doctors and energy healers, following diet plans, and taking supplements, Rachel was still in much pain, physically and emotionally.

> "The NB sessions helped me make sense of my life. I started feeling alive. That was the first time in five years where I felt a little lighter about everything. I wasn't in that deep, dark, bad place anymore." (Rachel)

I am an NB-certified specialist and authorized instructor, and I love what I do. NB allows my clients to find more balance in their lives, reach new goals and be healthier. Sometimes I feel fortunate, as I get to witness amazing miracles. The story I'm writing about is one of those. This story gives us a glimpse of what the body can do when given a chance to tell us what it wants.

In NB, there are no one-size-fits-all protocols. Every session is custom-made. By whom? By the client! All I need to do is ask the right questions in the suitable format, and the client (via muscle monitoring) will tell me exactly which procedures to use in the session and which homework to assign.

As an NB practitioner, the challenge is to put everything I know on the side and pay attention to the client's choices. Sometimes I have a hard time trusting the "client's muscle." After all, I have a lot of information about different health issues, the anatomy of the body, and how the body works. I sometimes want to base my decisions or treatment plan on that. But, as you will see in the story, that doesn't work.

Rachel, my client in this story, went to other "such types" of healers without any results. She says, *"Despite over five years of therapy, 18 months of journaling, seeing doctors and energy healers, following diet plans, and taking supplements, I was still in so much pain, physically and emotionally."*

When clients come to me, I need to remember it's not about giving them advice or information. It's about proper and careful muscle monitoring. For Rachel, the muscle monitoring made a difference right away. She recalls:

"After my first session of NB, I felt for the first time that the black cloud lifted. I was so free! My life started to make sense. In this short amount of time, I was able to heal so fast."

Rachel came to see me in November 2019 about a rash on her right shin that she tried to get rid of for about three years. As she walked in, I noticed a certain quietness about her, as if her body were harboring a deep, dark secret that she needed to protect. Interestingly, I got the feeling that this secret protected her.

In a very composed and gentle manner, Rachel explained how the rash tormented her and did not give her any peace. As I did the intake form during her initial visit, Rachel relayed that her dermatologist diagnosed the rash as eczema and prescribed very heavy steroids.

Rachel describes the effect of the steroids:

"It cleared up the rash, so I stopped using it. But after a few weeks, it came back three times as bad. So, I used the cream again, and it cleared up. Yet, when I stopped using it, it came back even worse. My skin constantly oozed and itched. I felt like the doctor couldn't help me. I had no clue.

At that time, I noticed an ad in the paper about a wound healing center that helps patients who suffer from eczema and similar skin conditions. So I decided to try it. At the wound healing center, the woman looked at the rash and explained that it looked like a bad reaction to the very heavy steroids. She told me to stop using the cream and that the rash would probably clear up. The rash cleared up after a few weeks but unfortunately returned. At that point, I knew I had to turn to holistic healing."

I felt bad for Rachel. I wanted to help her, yet I knew that it could be quite a challenge to get rid of eczema. Also, she worked on this issue for quite a while, and I did not know if I would help her.

During our first session, an exciting correction came up. As NB Specialists, we are taught that what comes up does not have to make sense; we do not have to understand why the body chooses a specific correction. With this in mind, we did a Phantom Sensation correction. Rachel had to hold the pad of her left pinky over the right tibia. We usually use this correction when something was removed from the body; so, I asked Rachel if she ever had surgery to have something removed from her body. To my surprise, she said, "Yes, I had a tumor in my right tibia and had the bone removed when I was 11 years old. It's in the same area of my rash."

It felt so good to hear this validation, and it made me feel more confident. I wasn't blindly choosing corrections for eczema; I knew that I was working on something a lot bigger.

After that correction, we did a Membrane Configuration:
— Feeling receiving love.

Rachel remembered that she never received love as a child. Instead, while she was growing up, people constantly told her that she was fat and that fat people cannot be successful as they have no place in this world. "Fat people just clog up our universe" were the words she always heard.

Rachel knew that the rash tried to tell her something. So her journaling therapy facilitator instructed her to have a conversation with the inflammation. The rash told her she was not attractive. However, at that point in time, Rachel ate very healthily and lost a lot of weight.

Rachel explains what she finally realized:

"I wasn't the fat person I'd always been anymore. As children, we believe what we are told. That's when I went through an identity crisis: if I'm not fat and I can't be beautiful, I know that I must be ugly. Through my journaling, I found out that I needed to have that eczema; I needed the rash to make me feel ugly and unattractive. It was like a crutch because it allowed me to keep my identity."

After hearing this, I realized Rachel was on a journey and needed a lot of help and support. I was aware of not giving her much time as I had a full practice, plus I taught NB. I did not have another slot open for at least three months; so, I muscle tested a plan to help her in the interim.

Since Rachel enjoyed journaling, I recommended she see my daughter, a Creative Journaling Expressive Arts facilitator, and complete her program called "The Recovery of Your Inner Child." I also tested that it would be beneficial to use the Bach flower remedy, Mustard. As she left my office, Rachel looked calmer, happier, and more confident. I felt that we were on the right track.

A few weeks later, I bumped into Rachel. She told me that her rash went away. But her healing was so much more profound than just the rash disappearing. For Rachel, that first session changed her life.

She shares the change:

"Those bioenergy corrections helped me make sense of what was going on in my life. As soon as the rash started clearing, I started feeling very light emotionally. My therapist tried to help me feel good about myself, but the constant itchiness and oozing made me feel ugly and unattractive. I couldn't even be intimate with my husband because I felt so horrible about myself.

After my NB session, I felt like a dark cloud was lifted. I was able to think that maybe I am beautiful. Perhaps the messages I got during my childhood were wrong. Yet, the thought that I was never loved was still excruciating. I cried a lot. Every time I became filled with these negative emotions, I used the Mustard remedy, which helped me. Mustard enabled me to be more accepting of myself and less judgmental of what I felt."

The night before she came to see me about her rash, she suddenly recalled a memory of when she was dating her husband. At that point, she wasn't sure if he was the man she wanted to marry.

"A close relative of mine said, 'He's tall and thin. This is your chance in life; this is your only chance to get married.' That person made me feel like this was my only opportunity to be worth anything. I realized that this person never cared about me; all he cared about was the outside—that I should look thin and beautiful. This caused me such crazy pain and hurt. It was too much; I felt like I was going to have a nervous breakdown. It was terrifying, I felt it in my whole body. Not just emotionally. I felt it physically. I was crying real bloody tears. I had to stop myself and come back to the present because I felt like I wasn't going to survive. I was in a dark, sad place when I came to see you."

This happens very often. Sometimes the client or I have thoughts or memories a night before the session. It is like the body energetically prepares for the session ahead. It is almost like the body already knows what the session will be about, and it gets ready to embark on the healing journey. The body stores all its traumas and memories on a cellular level. When prepared to face the truth, the body will release those cellular memories and bring them from the unconscious or subconscious to the conscious mind.

Rachel describes her feelings about coming out of her dark past:

"After that first session, I went into a much better headspace about my whole childhood. I still grieved, but I let go a little bit and started feeling alive. I felt that I could actually go on and make a new life for myself. That was the first time in five years where I felt a little lighter about everything, that I wasn't in that deep, dark, bad place anymore. I started to feel like I was coming out of it."

Rachel was due to see me in February 2020. Unfortunately, due to the COVID-19 lockdown, I didn't get to see her until July 2020, when the restrictions were lifted. As she came in for her second session, I was happy to see her looking so much lighter, more comfortable and healthier. She was in a much better place about her past, and we worked on her goals for the future.

Rachel is a certified yoga instructor but had a lot of confusion about her yoga journey. She questioned whether this was her actual life path. After her second NB session, she realized that she had a lot to offer to the world.

Rachel explains her realization:

"I started realizing that doing yoga doesn't interfere with my other desires or other talents. At this point in my life, it makes sense. I thought about dedicating my life to a career in fashion and design for women in the past. The NB work brought me to a much different place than anything else ever took me. I realized that by working on healing the body through yoga and health, I could help women feel more beautiful. It doesn't have to be through fashion and design. I also realized that my main focus now is to be a devoted, caring mother and wife, and yoga gives me that flexibility in my schedule."

Today, Rachel is totally healed from her rash. She is a successful yoga instructor and is living a happier life. She is passionate about healing, trauma release, and helping women feel better about themselves. In her words: "I am feeling so much lighter!"

About the Author

Judy Friedman is an NB-certified specialist and authorized instructor. With over two decades' experience, she loves serving the Monsey, New York community. The clients that she treated as eight-year-olds now bring their own eight-year-olds for sessions. What started as a practice for young families evolved into a massive business of having a large clientele of mature families and friends.

Judy now trains new students to help fill the needs of the Monsey community. "It's impossible for me to do this by myself," she says. "NB is so popular here. People love it. They feel it's the most fun way to heal."

Judy has a passion for studying and learning; she mastered many different modalities, which she brings into her practice. As an LMT, she enjoys incorporating some bodywork like CST, SER, Reiki, and Shiatsu into her sessions. "It's a beautiful way to end the session," she comments. "Yet my clients always want the NB. It gives them so much clarity about themselves and helps them overcome their obstacles and find their inner resources."

Contact Judy at sessionswithyitty@gmail.com.

Body, Mind, Spirit—and Heart

Cheryl Hannah Nicholson

Shane had cancer, chemotherapy, a bone marrow transplant, heart attacks, and underwent a heart transplant. As a result, he experienced PTSD because of what he describes as "all kinds of emotional crap." In addition, a lot of personality changes occur with a heart transplant because of taking another person's energy into your body along with aspects of the donor's personality stored in their heart.

> *"My cardiologist figured out what damaged my heart. In the end, I had four heart attacks. The doctors said, "Your heart's done, and you're done. You need a transplant. I could not have recovered physically and mentally as well as I did without Natural Bioenergetics." (Shane)*

Shane and I met 12 years ago when I ran a booth promoting my NB business at the local agricultural fair. He was fascinated with what I was doing and the accuracy of my answers in just a few minutes we had to work together.

Shane presented with a complex history of health issues

involving cancer and heart problems. He worked earlier with a naturopath, costing him $5,000 a month in supplements, but it did not help. He admitted that they might even have done some damage to his heart. During our initial meeting at the Agro Fair, I told Shane the priority items for him, as indicated after conducting muscle testing. This was quite a bit different from anything he experienced before.

In January 2000, Shane had been diagnosed with non-Hodgkin's lymphoma (a blood cancer) and a very rare form of bone cancer, which only five other people on the entire planet had in that time period. The treatment included radiation, chemotherapy, and a bone marrow transplant. This was brutal. They used a Hickman line that put chemotherapy into the heart because the chemo was so intense that it would destroy his arm. What they didn't tell Shane was that the chemo would destroy his heart instead.

Ten years later, Shane had his first heart attack. Ironically, he went to an exercise Boot Camp and was in excellent shape; but he ended up with a heart attack, and the doctors couldn't figure out why. They asked his wife, Lorin if he took any drugs like cocaine because his blood work didn't make sense, and the only reason they could think of for Shane having a heart attack was an overdose of cocaine. They sent him to St. Paul's Hospital, 500 miles away in Vancouver, British Columbia. They inserted a couple of heart stents, but they didn't know what else to do. Then they sent him home, where he suffered a second heart attack. That one was worse, a lot worse.

The doctors did more research and discovered that 80 percent of people given the Hickman line for delivering chemotherapy died suddenly from a heart attack.

Shane recalls:

"I give my cardiologist a lot of credit; he started the research to figure out what was going on. He was the one who figured out what damaged my heart. In the end, I had four heart attacks. The doctors said, 'Your heart's

done, and you're done. You need a transplant.'

They put me on an LVAD (Left Ventricular Assist Device), a mechanical pump that's implanted inside a person's chest to help a weakened heart pump blood, hoping to buy time to find a heart."

Typically, an LVAD lasts one to three years. Before Shane's surgery, we did a lot of work preparing his body to make sure the procedure and recovery would be as smooth and quick as possible. When Shane received the LVAD implant, the doctors said he would be in the hospital recovering for three months. But they sent him home after two! Shane still holds the record for the fastest recovery from an LVAD procedure.

Shane recalls:

"Two months was extremely rare. I credit part of that speed to NB, with Cheryl doing remote stuff, as well as working on me when she came down to visit. That really, really helped."

Shane then had to wait for a heart to be available and expected a three-year wait. Instead, less than three months later, he got the call: "Shane, we have a heart for you. You need to get down here right away!" Shane recalls the shock of that news and the following steps:

"We were so shocked! It wasn't even on our radar; so, we weren't prepared for it at all. We weren't packed, we weren't anything—and we had to be on a plane in less than 45 minutes. The shock was so big. We couldn't think straight. I packed a suit, shirt, a tie, no shoes, dress socks and a couple of pairs of underwear. The heart transplant team called the airport and asked them to hold the plane for us, which they did. In less than 45 minutes, we were flying to Vancouver. They got us all situated that night and told me that I would have the heart transplant in the morning."

At that time, the transplant crew, consisting of four doctors and nurses, a counselor, chaplain, and social worker, flew five hours across the country to Toronto to talk about Shane as a heart transplant recipient. He was the feature presentation at a big heart convention for doctors worldwide because of how unique his history and recovery was.

Shane's transplant crew was landing in Toronto for the conference when the call came in. They had to get right back on another plane to fly back to Vancouver so they could do Shane's heart transplant in the morning. The donor was being kept alive because the transplant team wasn't even in town.

Shane describes the emotional hit he felt before the transplant:

"The heart transplant itself was extremely hard, even just going into it. It's a flip of a coin – there's a 50 percent chance of dying and an 80 percent chance that once they open you up, they won't proceed. It was so challenging emotionally and mentally.

When you're going into a transplant, there's so much they don't tell you, which I think is an actual crime. It's not until I joined a Facebook community for transplant survivors that I realized I wasn't going crazy and others experienced the same challenges."

Shane woke up in the recovery room and didn't know if he had received the transplant or not. Shane's first thought when he woke up was, "Good, I'm still alive." He had to ask the nurse, "Did I get the transplant?" The nurse said, "Shane, you did. Everything went very smoothly. You're OK. I've got you. Just go back to sleep." Shane told me later that the nurse's words were like words from heaven, and her tone of voice was so sweet. "It was like the voice of an angel."

After the transplant, the process of recovery was regimented. He explains how NB and my working with him during his recovery helped.

"I remember there were a lot of things Cheryl worked on before the surgery, trying to stabilize my heart, and my emotions especially, because it was really hard going from hiking and doing all kinds of physical activity to a heart attack, to an LVAD, to a transplant so quickly. Cheryl helped me with PTSD because I got hit with all kinds of emotional crap once I had a moment to rest. It just overwhelmed me.

I knew Cheryl was working on me remotely because the first thing I wanted to do was see if I could sit up. I actually stood up two days post-transplant. The staff was like, 'Whoa! What are you doing?' I responded, 'When can I start walking?' They said it would be a couple of weeks. So, I said, 'OK, great, let's start that tomorrow.' The next day, I walked to the end of my room, and then a couple of days later, I walked to the end of the hallway. The staff were like, 'What is going on?'"

I got a phone call from Lorin two days after the transplant. She told me Shane was a little concerned because his oxygen levels dropped when he stood up, and he wondered why that would be. I replied, "He just had a heart transplant two days ago, right? He's not Mr. Potato Head. They don't just pop in and out that easily!"

Typically, people don't come out of anesthesia for at least a week; there he was, two days later, standing and starting to walk.

Shane explains he was a record-breaker:

"I broke every recovery record they have to this day. I know that because the last time I went to the heart transplant clinic, one of the nurses said, 'You're Shane; I heard about you. You broke a record, and to this day, you still hold it for recovery from the LVAD procedure, the transplant, everything. You still hold it.'"

His miraculous speed of recovery continued. The doctors said it would be a minimum of three months in Vancouver before they would even consider letting him take the 500-mile trip home, to which Shane said, "OK, so can I go home for Christmas? That's only two months away." On Christmas Eve, Shane and Lorin drove home. They sat in their home with a little battery-operated Christmas tree only six inches tall.

"We had no presents, nothing. But we plugged that little tree in, and that was the happiest Christmas we ever had. Two months after my transplant, I was sitting at home—that was unheard of."

The whole time Shane went through the process of surgery and then the recovery period, he followed the same protocols doctors usually advise every person to do. But Shane broke the records. So I asked him if there was anything he did that differed from other patients, and he responded:

"The only difference I had, compared to any other patient, was that I was working with you. I had the same training, with the same recovery, the same nurses and doctors, same drugs and protocols, same everything as other patients. The NB work was really the only difference."

I asked Shane to explain what he thought was the most profound work and aspect of NB:

"I don't even know if I can articulate it in a simple way. I think it was how natural it was. Some people thought it was all a bunch of baloney or just placebo. It doesn't matter if it was a placebo or not; the point is, it worked. There were no negative side effects to energy work, unlike drugs; with drugs, the side effects for most people are horrendous. One of the main benefits was that I didn't have to worry about that. I didn't have to go online to find out what I should expect in terms of negative side effects.

In some ways, because Cheryl and I worked together for so long, nothing surprises me anymore. I had extraordinary results the doctors couldn't account for in terms of how I did and how I recovered. Even so, I would say the biggest benefit of NB was the lack of negative side effects. There was no downside."

Shane still experiences PTSD. Doctors don't warn people that they likely will hit a wall of depression or experience a tremendous amount of guilt after having a transplant. Shane found that very difficult. There are also many personality changes with a heart transplant, as it puts another person's energy into the patient's body. There is a time period for transplant patients, especially in the first few years, where they don't know who they are because they don't feel or act the same way as before. It is bizarre. The transplant patient takes on some of the personality of the donor.

"I know my heart donor was a young man who passed away from a catastrophic motorcycle accident. He must have been good with the ladies because, on my first meal with my wife at a nice restaurant after the transplant, a beautiful waitress came to serve our table. My wife sat across from me, and I started hitting on the waitress. I said and did things I would never normally do, especially with my wife there. The funny thing is that it was like I was watching a movie outside of me. I suddenly came to my senses, realized what was happening, and thought, 'Where the hell did that come from?' I felt so bad for Lorin. She knew it wasn't me because that's not what I do. I was always respectful of her and other women. This guy was something else! Cheryl helped me with that because it was out of control—he was out of control."

I remember working on Shane one day, and I noticed a weird energy pattern on his torso. I ended up removing it because it looked and felt wrong. The following week, he told me about his issues with wanting to hit on other women and how it stopped cold once I removed that energy pattern.

Then there was the time Shane went to one of Tom Cruise's "Mission Impossible" movies. There is a scene in a luxury hotel where the window explodes out, and you're looking down what feels like four billion feet. Shane is not afraid of heights; he's a mountaineer, so he does a lot of rock climbing. But he was panicked at that scene! He reported sitting there thinking,

"What the hell is going on?" He said his heart raced at what felt like 4,000 BPM. He was sweating and suddenly was afraid of heights. Where did that come from? It was bizarre. He began recognizing new personality traits that he didn't have before.

I had to work at integrating both energy systems to work together in the same body. There is a mini-brain in the heart that actually has memory. Interestingly enough, Shane wanted to get a motorcycle before the heart transplant. After the transplant, no way! The donor himself did not want to ride a motorbike.

Shane describes our working together on getting both systems to work in the same body:

"It took us about a good five years of working together to get settled where I feel like I'm here and he's here. It's not like he takes over, and I feel like I'm an outsider in my own body. We go back and forth, but we work together."

After I read "The Heart's Code," I realized this is a common issue by Dr. Paul Pearsall, a doctor who observed this phenomenon in his patients. So, knowing Shane would lose some physical memory from his own heart, one of the things we attempted to do before the surgery was to download his hearts' information to other parts of his system, so that we could pull it back in after the transplant.

The one thing that really surprised Shane was his depression because of "survivor's guilt" that somebody had to die for him to live.

Shane describes this emotional challenge:

"That messed with me. We hear about heart transplant patients committing suicide because they can't deal with the guilt. It's so hard.

I was in the elevator where we were staying after the transplant. A lady in the elevator looked at me and asked, 'How long?' I replied, 'What do you mean?' She elaborated, 'How long since you had your transplant?'

Surprised, I asked her how she knew. She was a heart transplant surgeon from Europe and saw the staples coming out of the top of my chest. She said, 'I know that look. I know what you are going through. Congratulations!'

I was very appreciative of what she said, but it hit me about five minutes later: what do I get to be congratulated for? That I didn't die and someone else did? How do you process that? Intellectually, I understand that I was not responsible for his death. Still, the emotions are so hard to deal with because I have someone literally living inside me via his heart. Emotionally, it is probably the most difficult thing that I faced.

Cheryl was the only person able to help me process some of this. I couldn't go to my doctor because he had even less ability to do something about it. I could only pray about it. She validated my feelings by saying, 'Well, that makes sense because xyz,' and she showed me conclusions in the research she did. I would go to her with a problem and she would say, 'OK, let me get back to you on that.' It confirmed that I was not crazy."

A lot of the time, I didn't have answers for Shane at first. But because Natural Bioenergetics works, all I had to do was ask his body what it needed or what the issue was, and his body's muscle response told me the answer. Renowned psychoanalyst Carl Jung once said that there are many unconscious things that one cannot deal with until bringing them into conscious awareness. A lot of my work with Shane was about bringing up what we didn't know. We knew something was there, but we didn't know what it was until we asked the questions.

Shane still struggles with the sense that something emotional is going on under the surface, but he doesn't know what it is.

Shane explains how this feels:

"Normally, people know when they are mad and when they are happy. But what do you do with an emotion that has no category? I never felt that way before. It's like having a fruit that's never been grown before or seeing

a color that's never been seen. How do I describe something that I never felt before? Cheryl was able to bring this forward and say, 'OK, well this is what's going on....'"

One of the things we discovered through NB was that the heart transplant donor was angry; Shane had to deal with that because now he was angry too! We cannot blame the donor; he enjoyed his life, and, suddenly, boom! He currently lives in Shane, and the two were not getting along well. The donor, who was 22 when he died, wanted to be out doing what young kids were doing. But Shane was 48; so, the heart donor ended up inside a person more than twice his age. This sounds bizarre, but if you listen to enough heart transplant patients, it's their world.

Shane says one of the best aspects of this whole time was knowing that his wife, Lorin, was also taken care of. He acknowledges that he could not have gotten through this experience without her and that she could not have helped him as well as she has without the work I did to help her too. Lorin was an integral part of Shane's recovery and ongoing wellness.

Lorin shares her memory of how we helped her during Shane's challenges:

"From the beginning of this journey with Shane's heart attacks, Cheryl was right there for me, even with a phone call, to help in whatever way she could. When they flew Shane down to St. Paul's Hospital, Cheryl's treatments calmed me down. When he had his second heart attack, I was in so much shock, and she just took care of me. I had to get things organized for going to Vancouver for the transplant, and the whole time, Cheryl tapped into my energy and worked on me so that I could get things done and think clearly. The stress made my chest feel so heavy, but after her work with the magnets and the different positions and the points we held, it released all that pent-up energy I carried. At the same time, she was there to listen to me and often gave me a different perspective to consider as to what was happening. I don't think I could have gotten through this as well as I did without this work."

I want to thank Shane and Lorin for letting me share their difficult journey with you and allowing me to be a part of their story. As an NB Specialist, I learned, stretched, grew, and deepened my work by journeying with Shane and Lorin through this incredible experience. As so often happens, our clients are our most profound teachers.

About the Author

In 2002, Cheryl Hannah Nicholson was ill with a systemic yeast infection covering her entire body with an extremely itchy, raised red rash and the onset of allergies to food, animals, and more. This crisis launched her journey into the world of energy medicine.

In the summer of 2003, with a six-week-old baby in tow, Cheryl took an intensive course in Kinesionics, six days a week for the entirety of the summer. She did all her clinicals, wrote her exams, and became certified in Kinesionics. A friend insisted she needed to learn Natural Bioenergetics, so she started training in late 2010.

Now a Certified Natural Bioenergetics Specialist and teacher, Cheryl's chief joys, besides working with clients, are to mentor new students. NB allows her to successfully work on a wide range of conditions and imbalances with people worldwide. People easily connect with her because of her background in natural healing, herbalism, natural childbirth, and doula work.

Contact Cheryl Hannah Nicholson
Email: kinesionics@shaw.ca
Cell: 250-552-3495
https://www.kinesionics.ca/

Anxieties of a Vitamin Junkie

Franky Kossy

Abe had panic attacks and suffered from anxiety and paranoia. He was at the end of his rope and needed to find some answers.

"I felt utterly exhausted all the time and struggled to find strength, as I experienced brain fog and anxiety at the same time. The worst part was that it felt hellish coping with life itself." (Abe)

I leaped into Natural Bioenergetics in the year 2000 from a successful career in business, and it still never ceases to amaze me how excellent and how powerful this system of healing is. It is an effective and straightforward therapy and yet delivers the most life-changing results imaginable. Working with clients is akin to being a taxi driver because you start at a different place in your client's life, and you end up somewhere new each time.

I now share with you the story of Abe, a remarkable man on his quest for health and happiness.

Abe looked for a kinesiology "dude" and made an appointment

with me. I've been called many things in my life, but no one ever called me "dude" before. Somewhere in his search for self-healing, he read a book about such a "dude" who could use muscle response testing to decipher if something was good or harmful. As I was a Harley Street practitioner (a notable London location for medical practitioners); he figured I must know what I was doing as Harley Street practitioners are meant to be the best in their field.

Abe entered my office loaded down with two huge knapsacks, leading me to believe he was coming back from or going away on a trip. He sat down and heavy-heartedly started to pour out his story. He was a thirty-something musician cut down at his prime due to what he diagnosed as mercury poisoning from too many amalgam fillings.

He proceeded to tell me that his life was like being on a merry-go-round as he searched for answers as to why he felt so ill all the time. He removed his amalgam fillings and moved out of a damp apartment but was only marginally better. He then found an integrated medical doctor, who put him on a detoxification program using supplements. To my surprise, the two knapsacks were full of those recommended supplements.

Abe was so confused and no longer felt he knew whether his remedies worked or not. He wanted a kinesiology "dude" to check out the supplements and give him more guidance. On top of that. He told me he felt flat, was tired all the time, had panic attacks, and suffered from anxiety and paranoia since his university days. I could see he was at the end of his rope and needed to find some answers.

I proceeded (always guided by the muscle response testing) in a rather unusual way for a first meeting because I could see he needed to know why—despite all his efforts—he was unsuccessful at getting anywhere. We worked out why he felt the way he did and came up with the following results:
- 15% allergy-related problems
- 15% geopathic stress due to his environment
- 25% psychological issues

- 45% toxicity

Once I explained that the Natural Bioenergetics system prides itself on using body wisdom on how to proceed, we decided to follow that wisdom and hold off on checking the supplements at that time. I did an electromagnetic field correction using magnets and holding acupressure points to help his body systems come into alignment. Then he booked the next session.

Abe returned to my clinic a few weeks later with his knapsacks, but I could hardly believe it was the same man. He told me what happened after his first session.

"After that first session with you, I felt a massive change. I remember leaving your room and walking out of the building feeling drastically different. I felt the depth and calm around me at the same time. I noticed colors vividly, smells, noises, and people as if my senses were little by little waking up from a place of positive energy and regaining power. I felt I had strength in my legs again, and I remember feeling more myself. It was then I realized the scope of what Natural Bioenergetics could do.

"In only one session, I had such a powerful change, much more than all last years' efforts to get rid of the mercury poisoning. I said to myself after that session, 'OK! This is very important for me, and I want to experience more and also study this as a career and learn it so I can do it on myself and help others.'"

In the second consultation, we unpacked all his vitamins and supplements, and by placing each one on his body, we watched the reaction of his muscles. He was amazed that almost all but a few resulted in a weak muscle response (or no response) to the question, "Is Abe in any way, shape, or form benefiting from taking this?" It meant that Abe spent a lot of money on supplements that did not help him at all. He received no benefit from taking them!

He was delighted and relieved simultaneously because he

previously convinced himself he was incurable, as nothing had worked. We were ready to book another session and get on with the actual work outlined in the first session.

Over the subsequent two sessions, we worked on propping up his immune system with various Natural Bioenergetic techniques, one of which included his generating the following feelings and behaviors:
— *feeling insecure*
— *feeling rejected*
— *feeling abandoned*
— *behaving energetically*
— *behaving with self-confidence.*

The result of doing this correction (called a Membrane Configuration because it works at the level of the cell membrane) helped to eliminate the toxicity in his body. He seemed relatively quiet doing these techniques and afterward told me that he felt I dug out his dark secrets. I replied, "It wasn't me. You found these words; I consider myself a translator. The muscle response testing is simply my tool to help translate what your system needs for wellness."

In the same session, Abe had to think about these fears.
— *fear of life*
— *fear of being misunderstood*
— *fear of being seen*
— *fear of being inadequate*
— *fear of doing embarrassing things.*

It all made sense to him. I felt impressed that he related to and identified with the phrases. These fears, never once mentioned in any conversation, were part of the reason why he did not progress by just taking supplements.

Later, Abe confided in me that, before we started working together, his senses felt disassociated. He felt utterly exhausted all the time and struggled to find strength, as he experienced brain fog and anxiety at the same time. He said it felt "hellish" to cope with life basically.

Each time he returned, I saw that he was bouncier and more confident. He even told me that he started to feel a sense of ease in his relationship with his girlfriend; he said he felt closer and more connected to her than ever before.

On another occasion, we did a Symbiotic Energy Transformation, which cleared out the adverse effects of vaccines, heavy metals, radiation, and amalgam fillings. This was necessary because, although Abe previously removed all his amalgam and performed many detox programs, his body still carried the energetic pattern. This correction released the patterns entirely and gave him yet another breakthrough.

Abe confided in me again:

"I feel I have found my charisma and, in a way, I would say I got my 'mojo' back."

As a practitioner, it is an unusual feeling when a client's life transforms into what the person could only dream of before. I keep reminding myself that it is the client's effort with the help of a very precise and accurate system that enables that metamorphosis to occur. I get an incredible sense of satisfaction every time a client transforms, and I feel very privileged to have been a part of it.

I feel that Natural Bioenergetics is like taking apart a jigsaw puzzle to allow for a clean slate. This is what we give people who come to us: a clean slate to start again making healthy choices for a fulfilling life.

Abe expressed it succinctly:

"My ultimate goal by working together is to feel more alive and regain my true self, which was at some point disturbed. I definitely have a much more energized, brighter, and hopeful outlook on life. The powerful effect this therapy had on me still surprises me. I got my life back. It feels natural,

and I experienced the feeling of improvement as a smooth transition."

Abe and I still work together, but his goals changed. We continue to unpick the pieces of his puzzle.

About the Author

Franky is a professional Natural BioEnergetics Specialist and has been tutoring for over 15 years. She was awarded Tutor of the Year by the Federation of Holistic Therapists in 2015.

Franky was trained by Dr. Jimmy Scott and other senior, highly qualified practitioners. Her passion for both practicing and teaching sustained her for 20 years. She loves the newness of each group and is excited to be the wind behind her students' unique journeys.

She is a council member on the Natural BioEnergetics International Council and is involved in creating the teaching policies.

Franky runs a successful in-person practice in London's Harley Street and recently conducts her sessions remotely via Zoom video conferencing.

Book your session or take a class with Franky.
https://kinesiologycourse.com
franky@kinesiologycourse.com
https://www.youtube.com/channel/UCI3fgZvKR4Udz-_lIkhABhQ/videos

Peeling The Onion

Linda Orr Easthouse

Veronica had significant emotional and physical problems caused by her traumatic childhood and a complicated, abusive marriage. She experienced horrendous traumas and pretty much lost touch with herself. This is the story of how Natural Bioenergetics (NB) techniques helped her reset her life and achieve freedom and happiness.

> *"NB helped me to become me again!" (Veronica)*

I have been a Natural Bioenergetics Specialist in private practice, seeing clients full time since 2005. I am now the director of the Natural Bioenergetics Institute and lead the curriculum development team. This case study with Veronica illustrates the life-changing success she experienced through the deep and profound nature of this work.

Even after fifteen years, it still amazes me that what seems—from the outside—to be simple thoughts and small home routines can trigger fundamental changes in life. The process of communicating with the whole person through muscle monitoring and listening to what the body says gives voice to the deep, subconscious desires and needs of the person. This allows people to unwind the damage they suffered, layer after layer until they become themselves, whole and free.

I first encountered Veronica at a meeting where I spoke about my work at the Natural Bioenergetics Institute. She was a nervous wreck as she desperately tried to promote a failed small business. She came across to others as harsh, a little pushy, boastful but hollow. I did not want to buy in. The emotional baggage was everywhere. Afterward, she raved about my presentation and repeated how much she would love to work with me but that she just needed to get her business running first. I doubted I would see her again, so we left it at that.

A few weeks later, I ran into her at another meeting. It was clear that Veronica had some significant physical and emotional problems. Again, she mentioned that she would love to come and see me but did not want to book an appointment. This time, I took her name and number anyway and told her that I was an instructor.

When I teach, I sometimes need volunteers for students to practice on or for me to demonstrate a particular technique. So I told Veronica that she could get a little bit of work that wouldn't cost her anything and would at least be some help on her journey if she were interested in volunteering. She was delighted to do that.

So, Veronica became a demo body for my next class. This was a level-one class, with students just beginning their training. Even though it was a simple new technique for students, it was profound for Veronica. When I introduced Veronica, I told the students the little I knew about her background—just that she faced some problematic emotional situations at home.

The first correction I demonstrated was "Psychological Sentences." I used Veronica's arm muscle to illustrate how to choose what the body wanted to say. Then we demonstrated holding acupressure points until Veronica's energy system was at peace with her thoughts. Next, we did two simple sentences straight off the standard list:

— *I am respected.*
— *There is hope.*

Veronica recalls:

"*I was hugely overwhelmed by my living situation with a narcissistic husband. At the time, I didn't really know the ramifications or how deeply impactful it was on my life. I was really drained, stressed out, bloated, overweight, and continuing to gain weight steadily. Sleep was a big issue. I had very low self-esteem; my confidence was pretty much nil. I wasn't able to deal with the smallest of things and was not able to function very well in life. I had no respect, and I had no hope. Those seemed impossible.*"

As she shared her experience with the students, everyone was in tears. Veronica stayed to be a demo body for the practice group as well. They worked out some "Belief System Eliminations," including:
— *I love myself.*
— *I can't change.*

They also did a "Psychological I feel / I am" correction, using these emotions:
— *I feel wounded / I am needed.*

Veronica began to recognize some critical aspects of her life. Over the next two years, whenever I needed a body for a class, I called her, and she came. She benefited from these little bits and pieces of work done along the way. Through these experiences, her story came out, and she began to change her life.

Veronica came from a traumatic childhood and a challenging, abusive marriage. She reached the point where she had pretty much-lost touch with herself and did not know how to get out of her situation. But through the classes where she volunteered, she began to recognize what her real problems were. Crucially, she became willing to do something about it.

The demo corrections she experienced were all about the emotions around finding herself again, gaining the courage to do what she needed to do to protect herself, finding the agency and the voice to speak up for herself, and the firmness of mind to say, "No, I won't take this anymore."

Veronica says:

"I saw so much change through those little sessions. Someone understanding the situation and being able to help me meant I went from feeling hopeless to being hopeful."

She found the strength to make plans and put together a process for leaving the situation she was in.

At that point, Veronica began to have regular one-on-one sessions with me because things were moving forward. I really enjoyed working with Veronica because she understood it was about her and was willing to learn to take care of herself.

She began to do the energy work: She started doing the Meridian Tracing every day, reciting daily affirmations, and doing the NB Energy Toning Movements every day. She followed the diet and exercise required for life balance. Those actions gave her the strength to come back and do the hard emotional work.

From my perspective, it was fascinating to watch. As she began to do things for herself, she gained the ability to do what she had to do to end her relationship.

Veronica told me later:

"Your theory of love, acceptance, understanding, hopefulness and assurance meant I had the ability to know deep down that you were there. You knew exactly what was going on. I had the full gamut of support. As these changes started, I knew that I was not alone, that I was not the only one.

"With everything else I had tried, it was a little help here and something else there. But you understood the full picture - not just a slice of pie

here and a slice of pizza there. It was a no-brainer because I had the full scope—the whole circle, not just part of the circle. You really got what was going on for me. It was about what I wanted and needed, not some standard plan or pre-made program."

Veronica began to break the isolation she had been forced into through her abusive relationship. She found the courage to let go of the beliefs keeping her stuck. She examined and changed beliefs around "a marriage vow is sacred" and "breaking a vow is damnation." She realized that she was not in a "sacred marriage."

As we peeled back the layers of trauma, like the layers of an onion, she discovered her voice and began to name the actions in her marriage for what they were.

She found the words to admit that she was under an abuser who controlled her, and she was completely isolated from everyone and everything—and that it wasn't her fault. She found the words to acknowledge that she was not a bad person and did not deserve the abuse.

As we worked through the intense issues around abuse, allowing someone else to control so much of her life, and being stuck and unable to move forward, we broke through the paralysis so that Veronica could come out of her shell and reach out to those who could help her. She found a women's shelter and a lawyer and began to plan her escape.

Veronica recalls:

"It was hell. It was very difficult at the beginning and seemed undoable. But as I took baby steps, there were changes. I could do it! That was quite significant. Step by step, I just got it done. In the process, I learned about myself and how I wasn't in tune with myself and who I am. When I made up my mind, I could do it. That very thing was so deep for me. Every string we unraveled was important."

As we did the energy work, Veronica could stick to her decisions and follow through this time. So many people in abusive situations try to leave and then get sucked back in. Veronica had been on that roller coaster before. Still, as we did the work around self-beliefs (self-worth, self-image, forgiving herself, etc.), she gained courage and realized she no longer needed to stay in that relationship. No matter what her husband said, his actions demonstrated that he did not love her. She got off the rollercoaster, recognizing that her situation would not be different if she went back.

Veronica discovered she could support herself. She could be herself. She did not need to be in that abusive, isolated relationship and that she would be fine on her own. She would be better on her own. It was gratifying to see these changes over the matter of a couple of years.

Now looking back, Veronica explains how it made her feel:

"FREE! I feel free. During that time, I was watching my life change, becoming untangled and disconnected from the trauma. I was more liberated and able to handle life better.

"Initially, I found it so difficult to concentrate on the exercises you gave me and remembering such simple tracing was so difficult. I was always asking, 'How do you do this again?!' Implementing those difficult moves in the homework was very hard. I felt uncomfortable and didn't want to do it simply because it was a change. It seemed like so much change, especially with being in the state that I was in, was way too difficult for me. But I did it!

"And, oh, how it started shifting me, shifting my mindset and my heart. I'd say it brought me back to my center point. NB reset everything and opened my brainwaves and my intuitiveness. I became way more intuitive. I started to become me again.

"I was open to more things, more people, more events. I attracted good things into my life.

"Eventually, it came to the point of being able to leave my controlling,

manipulative, narcissistic husband. If I had just left, gone to counseling and the shelter, without the help from NB, I would have ended up back with my husband and probably would be dead by now. I would have fallen face-first again.

"There was no sustainability in facing my situation alone. With NB, I got to the root cause. Natural Bioenergetics digs up the roots; it digs up everything in your body, soul, and spirit.

"I lost so many years of life that I now want to tell other women: Stop doing it alone. Ask for help. Have a good support team. Ask for Natural Bioenergetics. It's really a no-brainer. This is a treatment that no one else has. There is no other type of treatment available like this. Your body is hardwired. And NB knows how to find that one wire, maybe more than a handful of wires, even if it's just one that is wired incorrectly or malfunctioning, NB can find it and change it. And that is worth more than anything. Do you really want to be free? This is the way to go."

Veronica continues to work her way forward with resolve and a clear mind. There are so many supports and pieces needed for women escaping abusive households, and Natural Bioenergetics gives them the internal fortitude and clarity to navigate and stick to the changes they need to make to achieve freedom and happiness.

Regardless of your trauma or situation, you need to address your internal stresses and traumas from a whole-person (body, mind, and soul) perspective. NB serves as the trunk around which all the other services contribute and integrate their part to support your transformation and regrowth to a vibrant woman able to support and care for herself.

I went through burnout before I found NB. Veronica experienced horrendous traumas, and NB is still unraveling the strings that bound her. What experience do you need unraveled? Contact me to begin the journey to freedom and wholeness.

About the Author

Linda Orr Easthouse is a stress management coach, energy medicine professional, radionics master, and best-selling author. With more than 15 years experience as a Natural Bioenergetics Specialist, she helps people change their patterns so that they can become whatever they want to be. Using therapies that restore the body, mind, and spirit, she assists people to take control of their stresses, establish healthy patterns, and gain control over their success and future. Many athletes and business owners seek her assistance to optimize their performance and outcomes.

Linda has a MA and many years of apprenticeship in the healing arts. She is the Director of the Natural Bioenergetics Institute. Her book, "Pushing the Reset Button: The busy professional's guide to a healthy lifestyle," made the Amazon bestseller list and has been sold around the world.

Contact Linda:
www.easthousecentre.com
www.naturalbioenergetics.ca
FB: ReClaimYourLifeCoaching
Instagram@lindaeasthouse
Email: Linda@Naturalbioenergetics.ca

Corrections for Allergy Suffering

David Schaffer

Rick suffered from debilitating seasonal allergies and had to take over-the-counter allergy pills daily to function during high-pollen days.

"It is amazing how connected our bodies really are. I had no idea that trauma can manifest physically in the body and create symptoms that modern medical science cannot fully explain." (Rick)

My wife Jamie and I were introduced to Natural Bioenergetics in 2014. After many visits as clients, an opportunity came up to learn the first three levels of NB. We both thought the timing was perfect for us and eagerly jumped right in. We were hooked after the first weekend of class and wanted to continue beyond the first three levels.

Initially, we thought this was something that we would learn to help ourselves, family members, and close friends. However, once we started learning the NB system, we could not stop learning! It was so exciting and unique that we wanted to share this with people who "fell through the cracks" of modern medicine.

It is exciting to see so many people respond positively and with curiosity to how our bodies want to find balance and healing. One of the first clients I began to see was Rick (not his real name).

The initial session that I did with Rick focused on ElectroMagnetic Field corrections using magnets and holding acupoints. This correction helps the body respond correctly to electric fields from outside the body. We also did an Electric Current correction using more magnets and holding acupoints to help the body correct some electric currents originating from inside the body, often caused by metals in teeth or other places.

Then we did a Belief System Elimination correction that involved "pinching" with one hand vertically on his forehead and horizontally on the base of his skull with the other hand while saying a phrase out loud for 30-60 seconds. Rick had to repeat one of the phrases while lightly pinching his forehead and base of the skull was "Authority is scary."

I vividly remember Rick's reaction to that correction. It was evident as it was written on his face. His entire countenance shifted. He looked at me and asked how I knew authority issues were part of his past. My response was, "I had no idea. I just know that your body was stressed by the belief that 'authority is scary' and your body wanted to deal with it today."

The first session concluded with four Membrane Configuration (MC) corrections. These corrections address, at the cellular level, the cell's ability to undo blockages while releasing toxins and allow nutrients to enter the cell for cellular health and vibrancy. One of the MCs that we did in the first session included "behaving: giving myself permission to love me."

Rick's reaction to the first few sessions was a mixture of skepticism and hopeful curiosity. He talked about something unique to the NB processes compared to all the other natural therapies he had tried, and he wanted to learn and experience more.

Rick stated:

"It is amazing that our bodies can physically manifest negative emotions and past hurts and traumas. Similar symptoms from both kinds of stress from past events and allergies can impact our physical well-being. Our bodies are truly amazing!"

We spent many sessions working on various physiological, emotional, and synergy corrections related to his allergies. Some of the emotional work that came up around the allergy reactions included:

— *Experiencing still*
— *Feeling worthless.*

He also worked to remove an old belief: "My parents didn't respect me."

Rick suffered from seasonal allergies. The area of south Texas where he lives is ripe with seasonal tree and grass pollen and heavy dust all year long. So he took one or two generic, over-the-counter allergy pills daily during the high-pollen days just to function and limp through the day.

One of the significant debilitating allergens included cedar pollen (Juniperus ash) that created cold-like symptoms such as varying degrees of painful sinus pressure, sneezing, and decreased respiratory lung function and capacity. We were able to do a correction (an SET correction), holding all six element endpoints along with a fresh-cut branch from a live cedar tree on his CV 6 (below his belly button) to give his body the right information to deal with the cedar pollen appropriately.

Rick recalls his situation prior to the NB sessions:

"I took daily generic allergy medication for over six years just to function and make it through the day. There were times my headaches and sinus were debilitating and increasingly annoying. It is amazing how our bodies can respond when given the correct information in a seemingly simple energy correction session.

Another significant change occurred in a home session that I was invited to do for Rick's family. Again, there was an opportunity to investigate some potential allergy work on the entire family around some flu-like symptoms lingering in the household.

After working out the synergy correction for the family, the second item I tested was Environmental Factors, specifically Geopathic Stress (*Geo* from the word Earth and *pathic* meaning feeling or suffering). This is an exciting category that deals with naturally occurring earth energies. Jane Thurnell Read wrote an entire book on this subject (*Geopathic Stress & Subtle Energy*). Her book gives an overview and testimonies of the changes she and other practitioners see while helping clients adjust and deal with naturally occurring earth energies.

To help Rick's family deal with the Geopathic stress negatively impacting them, I tested leaving a Life Transformer, a preprogrammed quartz crystal, taped on the inside door of the air conditioner closet upstairs in their home. I was a little perplexed at first with this particular little rock placement but I continued with the family session and worked through some psychological corrections.

At the end of the session, unbeknownst to me, Rick commented that their air conditioner gave them problems from the day they moved into their home. In fact, he told me that they had a service repair technician in their home, at minimum, every three months to try to diagnose and repair the unit that was only four years old. He even kept the receipts from all those service calls.

Rick recalls the results of the session:

"It is amazing the difference that the energy work and the little tiny rock made in our home! It has been three years since you did that work on our home, and I have not had to call for service or repair since you did whatever you did to our air conditioner. I saved thousands of dollars in repairs and service calls. It really is a remarkable change."

Rick continues to be an active client who returns for different issues, including back pain due to muscle strain from a busy lifestyle and many recreational activities.

Recently, he came for a painful back injury from wrestling with his children. In that session, we combined five items with five different magnets (ElectroMagnetic Fields corrections) on various spots on his mid and lower back while holding Cosbats (energy tools that include acupoints and provide an energy pattern for the body to use). We also did one psychological correction with him, thinking, "Being is what I have not."

His back pain was not immediately gone, although he left more relaxed than when he arrived at our office. However, over the next couple of days, Rick's body responded positively to the treatment, integrated the energy work, and he was back to his active work and busy lifestyle without pain.

Rick advocates that NB is a helpful and holistic way to view and look at traumas and injuries.

"I had no idea that trauma could manifest physically in the body and create symptoms that modern medical science cannot fully explain but only prescribe pharmaceuticals or costly specialist visits. I am grateful to experience the changes that NB provides and look forward to where else my body might benefit from more work."

Rick sent several family members and friends to visit our office to experience and see the difference that NB can make in people's lives.

Stories of change and healing like Rick's demonstrate that NB is a dynamic and powerful approach to helping people. We are so grateful that we can serve Rick, our family, and other clients with this valuable and robust modality of naturally healing the body. Natural Bioenergetics is a life-changing approach compared to modern medical treatments. Please contact us for help on any allergies symptoms you may be suffering from and other problems you might be facing. We would be happy to see if we can help!

About the Author

David Schaffer has a BA and MDIV degree in Theology, Leadership, and Bible. He worked as a pastor in churches for over 17 years. He and his wife Jamie completed their NB certification in 2018 and thoroughly enjoyed learning how effective NB is for their family and clients.

David is curious and wants to understand what changes clients feel and experience from their sessions. He wants to see clients grow and experience wholeness and wellness, making good healthy lifestyle choices.

Jamie is intuitive and detailed oriented with an artistic eye. Her clients appreciate her gentle and thorough approach. Together, Dave and Jamie run a home practice.

www.BalancedBioEnergetics.com
Email: SchafferBioEnergetics@gmail.com

Hit From Behind

Mary Beth Skellorn

Rosemary had throat symptoms and low energy levels. Due to an automobile accident, she also had pain in her right shoulder and arm. That pain increased with sharp stabbing, aching, and numbness that was so severe in her arm that at times she wished she could "cut it off."

> "I really wanted to get it resolved. I had been down all the other medical routes. By tapping into other areas through NB, you got to the bottom of it." (Rosemary)

I am a Natural Bioenergetics Specialist with 16 years professional experience working with clients of all ages. In this account, my client, Rosemary (not her real name), shares her story of working with me as she moved through trauma to regain comfort and normal function with the help of NB.

As you watch health unfolding for Rosemary, you will see the healing potential NB offers. I know from personal experience the joy of regaining my health with the help of my NB colleagues. So your healthier future is there for the asking.

Rosemary first came to see me in 2018 with digestive symptoms and pain in her left hip, right arm, and shoulder. Rosemary is a retired nurse who has used alternative treatments for many years. She knew of kinesiology and began learning about it via the internet but had never experienced it before.

In her first session, we worked together in person, with Rosemary lying on my treatment couch so that I could test a muscle in her lower arm. She recalls:

"I had been having discomfort in my lower left side and my abdomen just under my stomach, like a stitch, and some other gastric problems. I really wanted to get it resolved. As I had been down all the other routes, I wanted to see if kinesiology could help me."

Rosemary was surprised to find that the corrections her system selected via the muscle testing made connections between mental and emotional stresses and her physical symptoms and relieved both.

"I wasn't sure what to expect, although I knew a bit about it, and I knew there was muscle testing involved. It surprised me how it connected to all the elements, like the emotional side. I was feeling emotional at the time, I think, and going through some different things as well on the mental side and the physical side. I was surprised that by tapping into the muscles, you could actually get to the bottom of things, why I had those problems and hadn't been able to sort it out the medical way. By tapping into those other areas, you got to the bottom of it."

In the initial session, the corrections included ones where Rosemary had to think:
— *Fear that I am defective*
— *Self-growth / not self-growth*
— *Belong to the vital force.*

We did these corrections while holding the appropriate acupressure points to rebalance her system.

Rosemary said she was also surprised at the speed with which her system rebalanced itself after our first session. Within a week, both her hip and her digestive issues began to resolve.

"It surprised me how deeply it went on the emotional level. I was still surprised because I wanted to get results but also was a bit unsure or skeptical as well. It surprised me how you tapped into my emotional side and how I could be open with you in that way."

By the time of Rosemary's follow-up session after four weeks, the symptoms had been gone for so long that she forgot what she had been living with before her first treatment.

In 2020, Rosemary got in touch with me again, initially because she had an intermittent sore throat, and energy levels would drop sharply over the course of the day, leading to her falling asleep in a chair with her neck unsupported. This caused headaches and problems with pain in her right shoulder and arm.

We worked online in May during the coronavirus lockdown period, and I tested one of my muscles and acted as a surrogate for Rosemary. Also spent a bit of time discussing the history of problems with her right arm. At this point, Rosemary traced the issues back to a car accident in 2006.

Rosemary was stopped at a roundabout and about to start driving again into the traffic when she was hit solidly by another car from behind. The impact sent her car spinning across the junction. She was left severely shaken, with some whiplash and having hit her head at some point. Also, at first, she thought her right arm was broken.

The rebalancing work for Rosemary's throat symptoms, energy levels, and acute shoulder and right arm pain involved a series of vibrational essences that allowed the injured tissue areas to release unbalanced function and excessive sensory nerve impulses. She had two rebalancing thought corrections:

— *Fear for my safety*
— *Feeling criticized.*

At a follow-up session one month later, Rosemary's throat symptoms and low energy levels had resolved. But her right shoulder and arm became increasingly painful, with sharp stabbing, aching, and numbness so severe in her arm that at times she said she wished she could cut it off.

Rosemary describes the pain:

"I sought medical help, but even physio didn't resolve it. My arm could get to the stage where it felt numb, cold as if it didn't belong to me. Sometimes I just wanted to chop it off. It was so uncomfortable; it was driving me nuts."

The rebalancing work in this session addressed this "never been well since car accident/whiplash" state by rebalancing the meridian energy flows between a central vessel and kidney meridian, central vessel, and governing vessel, and the end-to-end flow along the liver meridian. This work released problems in Rosemary's central nervous system due to the emotions of fear and anger trapped in the physical tissues of the right shoulder and arm since the car accident in 2006.

When someone suffers a physical accident or trauma, the fear and upset experienced as part of the trauma can become lodged in the bodily tissue. This can make a complete recovery on a physical level difficult. Rosemary's memory of the accident informed the work we then did together. This memory enabled us to release the emotional and mental strain she experienced at the time of the accident and still carried in the physical tissues of her shoulder and arm.

The pain in Rosemary's shoulder went away very quickly after the session in June, as did all the numbness, tingling, and pain in her right arm. Her anxiety while driving since the accident meant that she continually checked her rear-view mirror for fear that something similar might occur again. She gradually realized she no longer thought about or checked what was happening behind her on the road and could concentrate adequately on where she was heading.

Rosemary explains:

"I still remember the accident quite clearly, you know, how it happened and where I was. It's still with me, but it's not so traumatic. I constantly looked in my rear-view mirror when driving to see who was coming up behind me because I feared it would happen again. Now that is gone, and I don't have that fear."

Rosemary says her right arm still aches at times, depending on how she uses it. But the sharp shoulder pain and the numbness and tingling have not returned.

On reading the account of our sessions and interview, Rosemary wrote the following account of her accident and its aftermath:

"Reading through what you wrote and what I said brings up things I never mentioned. I really don't know why it didn't come up.

When I had my accident in 2006, an ambulance, which was on its way to another call, stopped to help me. The traffic was completely held up by then. A witness told the ambulance driver that I was hit from behind with some force.

They called another ambulance to replace them so they could check me out. They put a collar on me in case I had any neck injuries, and they did not allow me out of the car, although I remember trying to get out. When the fire brigade arrived, I was cut out of the vehicle and then transferred to the A/E (ER) department at the local hospital. They checked me over and found no significant injuries.

My husband was at work, and he had to come and fetch me home. This was a particularly stressful time for me, as I was in the middle of studying for a degree, and my mother was unwell.

I remember the first day was not too bad. I just rested and took pain relief and anti-inflammatories. The next day, everything hit hard, as you would expect from whiplash. I remember that the strange sensation was known as allodynia (which is pain responding to a non-painful stimulus). When I touched my legs or arms, I felt pain, even with a light touch. I was also frightened to sneeze or cough because I didn't want to jar my neck. I already had a neck issue and didn't want to make it worse. My husband had to help me wash my hair, dress, etc. Every movement was painful.

I saw a general practitioner after two weeks just to check that all was well and explained that I was treating myself. I think it took two or three weeks for me to get back to some normality. I did not drive until then, as I was too scared. The allodynia went away after about a week, but it is hard to recall it. The accident was reported in the local paper. When I read it, I remember being very tearful.

After my sessions with you in May and June, my arm has been much better."

Rosemary is a reserved and gentle person. Nonetheless, at the end of our face-to-face sessions, she always asked if she could hug me. It is such a privilege to be a part of her rebalancing and recovery.

About the Author

Mary Beth Skellorn is a Natural Bioenergetics Specialist and a homeopathic practitioner. She works remotely from her home in Suffolk in the UK. Her search for personal health led her to homeopathy and then to Natural Bioenergetics (NB), which she has practiced with clients since 2004.

Mary Beth says NB is the most effective of all the alternatives she has tried, both as a client and practitioner. She is so grateful to have her life back and to be able to offer clients of all ages the very best road to the recovery of their vitality on every level, regardless of their initial goals or concerns.

Mary Beth's clients leave behind health problems of all kinds and use NB to improve practical skills or be organized, learn, and build confidence in work and social settings. She believes it is a privilege to see clients grow in skill and confidence who previously were held back by so many different things in their lives.

She says, "NB returned me to health, and it can do the same for you. I work from home and can find an appointment to suit your timetable. I'd like to help you, too."

marybeth@marybethskellorn.com
0044 (0)7765 828629
marybethskellorn.com

The Mind Does Not Like Pain

Brian L. Mathews

Sara had unrecognized turbulent experiences while growing up and stress and PTSD from 16 years serving as head nurse in the Cardiac Intensive Care unit at an inner-city hospital. These traumas eventually manifested in a significant physical crisis involving debilitating hives, spontaneous anaphylaxis, inflammation throughout her body, and violent vomiting from contact with gluten foods.

"I was at a point of complete desperation. I couldn't think deeper than that. The feeling of impending, imminent doom was so strong. I didn't understand all the pain I carried—until it left me by working through NB." (Sara)

When I first discovered Natural Bioenergetics in 2009, I saw seemingly impossible events begin to occur in people's lives. Debilitating, overwhelming pain and physical dysfunction simply began to go away. From the crippling effects of a ruptured disc to severe daily headaches resulting from a car accident to major food allergies affecting a child's development. It seemed that miracles occurred. I had no idea what Natural Bioenergetics was, but I intended to find out.

After attending the first course of NB training in 2010, I knew how I wanted to spend the rest of my life. So, upon completing training and certification in 2013, I opened my first office. I am now the co-owner of a company offering services in the field of complementary health and wellness. I work full time with clients locally, nationally, and internationally.

The following story of my client Sara's experience details a fascinating journey into the resilience of the human spirit and how miraculously the human biofield (body, mind and spirit) can recover from overwhelming trauma.

When Sara first came into my office in the spring of 2017, she seemed an incredibly intelligent and deeply knowledgeable person, but she obviously was in a major health crisis. Her knowledge of the physical body was enormous. She knew very clearly what was happening to her; however, neither she nor anyone else at that time could address the causal issues.

Sara said her body betrayed her and that she was out of resources to deal with what she experienced. On her client intake form, she listed concerns of autoimmunity (possibly celiac disease or lupus), allergies, hives, angioedema, and weight gain. She was taking megadoses of REACTINE to cope with these symptoms. While she focused on resolving these physical challenges, she also experienced the challenges of PTSD, caused by stress and anxiety in her previous career as a nurse.

Sara recalled her physical and mental condition when she came to her first session with me. She says she was at a point of "complete desperation" and "couldn't think deeper than that." After that, she says she was "generally in a total mental fog."

"There was nowhere else for me to go; otherwise, I would have been hospitalized and on prednisone. There was a potential diagnosis of lupus floating around. Also, I was allergic to outdoor mold, which is fun because I live in a rain forest! My most immediate issue was hives— debilitating

hives with spontaneous anaphylaxis, to be exact. It was not a mild problem; it was explosive. The hives were itchiness to the extreme. It was non-stop. My immediate need was to figure out how to stop the itchiness. I was willing to do whatever it took to make it stop. With the hives came a constant histamine flush in my face— redness and blotchiness.

I had a wicked hot skin breakout around my neck. And I was swollen everywhere; it was like everything was totally inflamed. I was like a giant hot air balloon! Food wasn't at the top of the list, but when I came into contact with gluten, that's when things got really bad."

In that first session, Sara was at such a heightened state of anxiety that her body began addressing imbalances while gently opening the door into the emotional pain buried deep inside.

We began with a BioEnergy Control System Membrane Configuration:
— Experiencing Serenity.
Then followed a group of Psychological Gerunds:
— Letting go of being in control
— Letting go of the necessity
— Letting go of responsibility
— Letting go of flawed.
She finished the session by updating her biofield's ability to recognize and address the toxic load of a few items with which she had contact. We used a Symbiotic Energy Transformation (SET) Correction:
— X-Ray
— Isopropyl Alcohol
— Iodine 131
— Chloroform
— Oil and solvent products.

Sara saw changes almost immediately. Over the next few weeks, she began "shedding puffiness" and experienced a significant increase in her energy levels. She also reduced her REAC-

TINE intake to a fraction of previous levels.

One of the fantastic things I look for when working with a client is when hope begins to appear. Hope is an amazing healer; it unlocks the hold fear can have on a person. As Sara continued to work through the sessions, she moved closer to the core emotional issues that heavily affected her physical state.

The emotional influence of her turbulent upbringing and the significant stress and anxiety of her previous career were about to be made known.

She describes the emotional turbulence she experienced in the session where her first memory came out.

"I began to understand the power of NB when the first memory came out. We had had a few sessions by then, so I had gained some trust in Brian and the process. It was such a traumatic memory! I remember thinking, 'Why does my mind want to think of that? I don't want to think about that memory.' I was beginning to panic because I didn't understand how this was going to present itself.

It felt like my body was literally saying, 'Like a volcano, this trauma is coming up.' It was so painful to get close to. I remember saying, 'I feel like there's an elephant sitting on my chest.' It felt like my life or death was happening right then. And then it literally lifted off my chest and was gone. I was so overwhelmed by the effectiveness of the NB process. Then the thought came into my mind" How many more of those traumas are in me?"

Sara described that memory as the bottleneck. She began to see what her NB journey would be about. She mustered all the courage she needed to be present and let her bodywork through the NB process; allowing herself to heal naturally, organically, and gently. Sara became so excited as she understood more and more of what was happening.

"I felt such relief—like I could breathe again. It was as if I'd been under a cloud that was constantly wrapped around me. I didn't understand that

I had been carrying all that pain until it left me. I felt very hopeful. As I lay on the table during our sessions, I could feel things. I thought, 'Something is happening here.' I might not be able to articulate it clearly, but I actually felt hope, and I trusted the process. I believed in NB."

As we continued to work together over the next several months, more of her story began to pour out. As we addressed the emotional pain, we moved to other more obvious physical issues. One of those issues was food.

Food has many meanings for a person. It can be very emotional. It can take us back to joyful memories; for example, the smell of cookies baking can transport us back to Grandma's kitchen when we were children. Or food can be terrifying; it can trigger thoughts of something painful or isolation from one's community.

In Sara's case, her physical reaction to gluten was shocking.

"If I ate any amount of gluten, the effect was swift and horrible. It would begin like a flood, like when the train had already left the station, and there's nothing that can be done to stop it. I had a 30-minute window before the effect began. The anxiety of what was coming would turn into panic. I would scramble, trying to prepare myself mentally for it. Then it would come, and I would lose my breath. Projectile vomiting would go on for 8-10 hours. I had difficulty breathing because there was no time to breathe because the vomiting was so fast and furious.

The feeling of impending, imminent doom was so strong. I was afraid that I would aspirate, choke, and die. I often ended up on my knees, passed out on a bathroom floor, and stayed like that for hours and hours, just totally passed out. It was so horrible; everyone left because it was so hard to witness. Then it would take me a week to recover.

I was a Registered Nurse for 22 years. For the last 16 years of my career, I worked as a head nurse in the Cardiac Intensive Care unit at a downtown inner-city hospital. I had anatomy and physiology knowledge, extensive training, and certificates for my degree in critical care nursing. The inten-

sive pathophysiological knowledge of the medical effects my gluten reactions had on my body was very specific. I carried that knowledge around with me, wondering how many more times I could go through this before my stomach would perforate and I would die. And no one was able to help me."

One of the things we understand in NB is that the body listens to the mind; if the mind is in crisis, the body will demonstrate that. Psychological and emotional trauma is remembered by the human biofield, even long after we have forgotten the event. Sara suffered significant trauma throughout her life that had not been recognized. Whether from words spoken or deeds done, a person remembers the impact of a traumatic event. When I work with a client, I ensure that person's journey is as gentle as it is powerful. It is a sacred thing to be trusted with a person's pain.

Through the months of our working together, it became more and more evident that Sara had an intelligent mind. During sessions in the months that followed the clearing of the bottleneck, she became more and more aware of the depth of herself and how profound it is to be human and have a biofield. Amid her journey, she finally understood a deep truth about the mind; it does not like pain.

Sara recalls the revelation she had about keeping and then letting go of painful memories in her mind.

"My body did all of the talking. I was like, 'Oh, it didn't even ask me for permission; it just did what it needed to do to be well.' My body was ready; it was handing Brian all the information needed, as if on a silver platter. Almost like my body was saying, 'Here, this is what's going on.'

I kept asking myself what was the opposing force that kept all that stuff inside my mind when my body was so willing to just give it over to Brian when asked. The opposing force was my subconscious. Pretty early on, I had a revelation that the brain really works hard to keep things stuffed down to avoid pain. But in the long run, that causes a lot of problems. I think that's when I realized how quickly this NB process worked. I didn't have to do 10,000 affirmations, tap my head 10,000 times, or do other things to bypass the subconscious. This process was so quick."

During our time working together, Sara worked with many different NB corrections and processes. Why so many? Because the human mind can handle 400,000,000 signals a second and filters that down through many systems to approximately seven different items that we can consciously handle at any given time. With such a vast amount of information moving through our systems, it's no wonder that stress, anxiety, and trauma have such an enormous effect on us.

When that harmful influence clears, the biofield can do wonders. We used many different NB corrections and processes to clear Sara's mind. The human biofield works in incredibly intricate ways. To address a physical issue, it uses psychological and emotional corrections, realigns electromagnetic fields, eliminates cellular toxicity to increase neuro-synaptic function, addresses sympathetic and parasympathetic misfiring, and much, much more.

I asked Sara to describe what she first learned about herself in the process of our working together. She says it took her to a "different level of enlightenment."

She further explains:

"You know how sometimes we hear that we're body, soul, and spirit? NB helped me gain that knowledge through a personal revelation of being body, soul, and spirit. I understood it at such a level that it actually humbled me. I realized I really need to pay attention to what's going on. I think the most significant factor that contributed to a lot of my physical symptoms was the PTSD from my nursing career.

I'm very different now. I worked through a lot of that in the process of working with NB. I was willing to go deeper. I feel like a new person."

Recently, I asked Sara for an update on her life as it is today. She shares how different it is:

"I don't have daily hives. I don't have anaphylaxis. I don't have a foggy brain. I don't have swelling. I've lost 60 pounds, even when I eat more food than I did before. I no longer react to gluten. I feel that my body works well, the way it's supposed to. My body, mind, and spirit function so synergistically that I feel more myself than ever before. My spiritual gifts have always been there, but now they work at quantum speed."

Sara adds her perspective on spirituality and wellness:

"I believe Natural Bioenergetics is very important because it opens a person up to the revelation about how spiritual we are as human beings. I think it scares people a little bit to know how spiritual they are. Everybody has gifts, and if we were all operating optimally and healthily, it blows my mind to think of how our world would function differently.

Remember, if you don't make time for your wellness, you'll be forced to make time for your illness. Your emotional and spiritual health are the most important things because they manifest your physical health."

The opportunities to witness and be a part of the incredible changes in Sara's life was a profound privilege for me.

About the Author

Brian L. Mathews is an Advanced Natural Bioenergetics Specialist and has been working in the field of energy medicine and stress elimination since 2013. He is passionate about working with individuals who are trapped by harmful habits, limiting beliefs, and traumatic life experiences. Brian uses a range of disciplines and techniques designed to restore the body, mind and spirit to optimal function. He has a strong reputation for supporting his clients in their journey towards freedom from the issues that stop them from becoming all they can be and living a life of joy and peace.

Brian is the President and Executive Director of Natural Bioenergetics Global, a Canadian not-for-profit organization that facilitates Natural Bioenergetic training worldwide. He is also Vice President of the NB Institute and sits on the NB International Council.

Contact Brian:
To schedule an appointment: Brian@bioenergeticbydesign.com.
Information regarding Natural Bioenergetics Global and the 100-year vision: Office@nbglobal.org

Removing the Fortress of Non-Protective Walls

Linda Orr Easthouse

Richard grew up in a very abusive situation. Later as an adult, he suffered depression, job loss, and relationship problems. He could barely get out of bed and function. He felt his body cry out in agony, and he felt he could no longer continue fighting the problems.

> "I want you to know it's possible. It's possible to heal from whatever is ailing you. It's possible to feel happy again. It's possible to break those chains of abuse. It's possible to heal your ancestral wounds. It's possible." (Richard)

As a Natural Bioenergetics Specialist, I find it so gratifying to play a part in a person's journey to wholeness, to be able to accompany someone through self-discovery of who and what they can be, regardless of what happened in the past. Healing of body, mind, and heart is available to each and every person.

I want to share an amazing story of recovery and self-discovery through NB. This is the story of someone who grew up in a very abusive situation. Every word of the following story is true.

It is a story that many men need to hear. I changed the names and places to protect anonymity. The following story is told in his own words.

"My name is Richard. I have a beautiful family of five and work full time as a manager at a nationally known business. I use Natural Bioenergetics to help myself, my family, and my friends. My family and I are all strong, happy, and healthy, though we were not always this way.

I grew up in a very strict religious household. We went to church to learn how God wanted us to act. 'Love thy neighbor as thyself. Honor your father and mother. Do unto others as you would have them do unto you." These teachings became very confusing for me as a young boy when my dad was a nice man at church and a monster at home.

I was physically, emotionally, and verbally abused until I finally protected myself at age 16. I still remember that day. The consequence of standing up for myself was getting kicked out and becoming homeless. I felt that no one would ever love me if my own family didn't.

For as long as I could remember, I suffered frequent bouts of immense sadness, agony, and night terrors. These were the repercussions of those many years of childhood abuse. The first time I remember wanting to die was when I was 12. I remember standing in the kitchen pushing a dull kitchen knife against my abdominal area.

As an adult, my sadness was very intense at times. There were days when I struggled to get out of bed. It took all my strength to go to work and act like everything was OK. I ended up losing two jobs because I could barely function. I struggled in my relationship with my wife and the people around me. Things got so bad that I started to think about ending my life again.

When I first discovered Natural Bioenergetics, I was fresh out of the hospital after reaching a breaking point. Not only did I feel like giving up and ending my life, but it felt like my body reached the point of wanting to give up as well. It felt like my body was crying out to me in agony. This scared me. I felt like I could no longer continue fighting, so I decided to ask for help.

For most of my life, the feelings of humiliation and shame kept me from seeking help. Depression wasn't really talked about, and men were supposed to remain strong; we were not supposed to show our feelings. Part of me thought I was stuck this way. I read self-help books and watched inspirational videos on the internet to give me strategies to keep pushing through. These tools only took the edge off; they kept my head above water, just about surviving.

After spending six days in a psychiatric hospital learning new life strategies and being put on a pretty high dose of antidepressants, I felt stable enough to go home.

I still remember my first session with a Natural Bioenergetic Specialist. During the session, I remember thinking 'this stuff is weird.' I thought, 'Is she asking me these questions, or someone else?'

After the session was finished, I felt like a brand new person. I felt an immense weight lift off my shoulders. It felt like all the sadness left my body. I was blown away; the experience was incredible.

I spent the next couple of months feeling great. Then, feelings of worry, sadness, and despair started to creep back. So, I went for my second session and had the same experience. I remember driving home and not being able to contain my smile.

One of the sessions focused on the issue "tired and down." Two of the energetic balancing corrections stood out because of how powerful they were. The first was a group of Psychological Inverted Structures:

— *Optimism about future I have not*
— *Blame I do not*
— *Limitations I do have.*

I believe these psychological inverted structures can be so powerful because they can reach energetic imbalances to which we don't normally have access. Dr. Jimmy Scott, founder and creator of the NB system, explains that, during the process, the conscious mind is briefly distracted or kept busy interpreting the meaning of the statement, simply distracting the body's protective functions long enough to balance the energetic disturbance.

This correction was dead on for me. At the time, I had no optimism for the future. I blamed my father for my struggles and had many limitations. I kept myself in a fortress of walls, keeping me safe from getting hurt again. So, I definitely needed the distraction.

The second group was Psychological Word Strings:
— *Scared sympathetic insecure anger jerk*
— *Alarm dream positivity admired isolating*
— *Controlling reassured death grateful.*

Dr. Jimmy Scott always warned about the power of word strings. He taught us to do no more than two or three at a time. I don't remember what this correction was about or how it was connected. I just remember it helped me let go of a lot of fear and stress very quickly. Not knowing is OK. We don't always have to have the answers. To protect us, sometimes our bodies will not allow us to remember what it was about.

Once I finally realized and trusted that Natural Bioenergetics was the answer to my prayers, that it could help me become the man I wanted to be, I committed to my healing journey. I not only wanted to become the man I was designed to be but also wanted to help others by becoming a Natural Bioenergetic Specialist.

After I completed the first course, I remember not practicing anything I'd learned for at least a year. It felt as if I had uncovered a wall that prevented me from moving forward, and I was scared to break it down to see what was on the other side. One day, I finally broke through and started the healing journey. I felt a strong motivation behind me, pushing me through. It was hard to stop, and I felt dedicated.

After only one year of working and training with Natural Bioenergetics, I completely weaned myself off antidepressants with the help of my doctor. This was a huge win for me, as I had achieved one of my goals. I noticed my relationship with my wife improved; I was a better father, friend, and employee.

Around the same time, I began to realize just how much damage happened to me when I was growing up. It did not stop there. There were, of course, the aftereffects of unhealthy coping skills including drinking, drugs, self-isolation, gambling, and smoking tobacco. As these issues came up and were released, I knew I was heading in the right direction.

During my training, I volunteered to demonstrate for the class a new technique called Age Identity. This is a balancing of an energy disturbance that we are not able to correct unless we go back to the time period of when the original energy disturbance took place.

The correction was done in two stages. The first took me back to the womb of my mother; the second was shortly after birth. I remember my whole body shaking and feeling sensations of heaviness, heavy emotions and struggles as I descended backwards in time. It occurred to me that I was passing through moments in time that were not resolved yet. When I reached my first destination, the shaking stopped, and I felt a calmness come over me.

During the rebalancing, I saw a vision of a child in a womb and immediately got a vision of a monster or devilish-looking face. As I explained my experience to the class, I had an aha moment. I remembered my mom telling me that she was in labor with me for 41 hours. She said she felt like I did not want to come out. I concluded that the vision of the baby was me and the vision of the monster was my father. I was too scared to come out and face the monster. After the rebalancing was complete, I felt calm and lighter.

An amazing benefit of working with Natural Bioenergetics is that, as I worked on certain problems, I noticed entirely different issues start to disappear. For example, I used to have night terrors every night for months at a time. My night terrors diminished to one every three to six months. I used to have symptoms similar to Post Traumatic Stress Disorder (PTSD), which are now completely gone. My seasonal allergies disappeared too.

As time went on, I noticed that at the same time every day I became agitated. One way of working on an issue is to find out how many factors contribute to the problem you want to resolve. I discovered that one of the contributing factors behind my agitation was feeling invisible. Throughout my life, I often felt invisible because, no matter how hard I worked at my job, I almost never received recognition for my hard work. Shortly after this NB session, my supervisor at work complimented on the great job I was doing. He did this twice in one week, plus the main boss thanked me for all my hard work.

Today, I can't imagine my life without Natural Bioenergetics. It has been truly life-changing for me and my family. The skills and knowledge I acquired and developed are unparalleled. Over the years, I noticed my family's relationships and health improved.

Most of us were taught that we must learn to live with our ill health and the patterns we inherited from our parents. Through NB, I learned how to do things that many of us were taught are impossible. My healing journey was not always easy. Sometimes, it was painful and scary. But it was also amazing and miraculous. At times, I felt like I would never make it to the finish line; but there were other times when I felt like I had won the race.

The reason I share my story with you is because you may have experienced a similar struggle or background. I want you to know it's possible to heal from whatever ails you. It's possible to feel happy again. It's possible to break those chains of abuse. It's possible to heal your ancestral wounds. It's possible. Just take it one step at a time. Ask for help.

Most importantly, keep moving forward and don't give up. Treat your healing journey as a way of life, like eating and drinking; and before you know it, you'll notice a new spring in your step.

I hope my story gives you strength, courage, and the motivation to make choices and allow change to happen in your life."

About the Author

Linda Orr Easthouse is a stress management coach, energy medicine professional, radionics master, and best-selling author. With more than 15 years' experience as a Natural Bioenergetics Specialist, she helps people change their patterns so that they can become whatever they want to be. Using therapies that restore the body, mind, and spirit, she assists people to take control of their stresses, establish healthy patterns, and gain control over their success and future. Many athletes and business owners seek her assistance to optimize their performance and outcomes.

Linda has a MA and many years of apprenticeship in the healing arts. She is the Director of the Natural Bioenergetics Institute. Her book, "Pushing the Reset Button: The busy professional's guide to a healthy lifestyle," made the Amazon best seller list and has been sold around the world.

Contact Linda
www.easthousecentre.com
www.naturalbioenergetics.ca
FB: ReClaimYourLifeCoaching
Instagram@lindaeasthouse
Email: Linda@Naturalbioenergetics.ca

From Hopeless to Hope and Happiness

Sharon Mathews

Vanessa felt hopeless and suffered a breakdown. She became completely overwhelmed and depressed. She experienced rashes, food insensitivities, headaches, viruses, fatigue, jaw pain, vertigo, and more. And her parents had to take care of her children.

"I think the worst part of all the emotional and physical struggle that I was going through was knowing the strain that I was putting on my family." (Vanessa)

I was first introduced to Natural Bioenergetics in 2009. For me, it was a last-ditch effort to deal with ongoing debilitating pain resulting from a back injury and a subsequent car accident. It was here that I discovered a gentle therapy that addressed not only the physical trauma, but incorporated emotional, mental, and spiritual health as well. As I began to improve in seemingly impossible ways, I decided I wanted to offer this amazing gentle, holistic therapy to others. I became certified in Natural Bioenergetics in 2013 and am now co-owner of a company that offers complementary health and wellness services locally, nationally, and internationally.

I had the privilege of being a part of the transformation of my client, Vanessa. Her story is inspirational and heartwarming. It is a story of hope and shows the courage and commitment of a young woman who did whatever it took to get her life back.

When I met Vanessa, she was at a very low place in her life. She describes that after the birth of her second child her anxiety "went through the roof!"

"I felt completely overwhelmed, depressed, and felt like I was never good enough as a mother, no matter how hard I tried. When my youngest was about a year old, I completely broke down. After this breakdown, I noticed strange food sensitivities that I never had before, various rashes and extreme fatigue. I also started to get every cold, flu, and virus that went around. In addition to all this, I started to experience horrendous headaches, earaches, and vertigo. My physical and emotional health was so bad that my parents had to help me take care of my kids as I was completely unable to do so. I also couldn't even drive because of vertigo and had virtually no energy to do anything."

Vanessa was referred to me by a Registered Holistic Nutritionist. The food she was able to eat became severely limited and, as they tried to reintroduce different foods, she reacted without any sign of getting better. Her nutritionist suggested that the food disorder could be emotional and referred her to me.

Although Vanessa had never heard of Natural Bioenergetics and did not understand how food sensitivities could be tied to emotions, she described that she was willing to give it a try because she "was so desperate, and nothing else seemed to be working."

Vanessa recalls:

"I was seeing a lot of specialists at this time to help deal with my various issues, and I was trying everything, from natural approaches, diets,

supplements, Chinese medicine to doctors, ENTs, and TMJ specialists. Nothing helped. I was SO hopeless."

My hope when I started working with Sharon was that I would be able to eat more food; that was it. I never even thought that it could help with any of the other physical or emotional issues I was dealing with."

During the first few appointments, I worked with Vanessa mainly on getting her energy stabilized so that she was at a place where her body actually had the energy to heal. We also addressed her reactions to a few foods, dust, cats, and grasses. She told me that she was so used to waking up tired and congested and just figured that was the way it was.

"When Sharon did some corrections on me, I was shocked to notice an immediate change the very next day! For the first time in years, I did not wake up congested and exhausted. I was so thrilled. Where we live, we had been getting some smoke from forest fires nearby in the summertime. Sharon did a correction for the smoke, and that helped a lot as well."

In conjunction with this, we worked around the stresses pertaining to certain needs:
— *Needing comfort*
— *Needing to have dreams*
— *Needing the despondency to go*
— *Needing acknowledgment*
— *Needing moral support.*

We also did some psychological work around fears:
— *Fear of being overwhelmed*
— *Fear that other people are better than me*
— *Fear that I will never fulfill my goals.*

These were all relevant corrections.
Vanessa describes her feelings at that time:

"I think the worst part of all the emotional and physical struggle that I went through was knowing the strain that I put on my family. My parents had to put their lives on hold to take care of my children, and my husband (who is self-employed and whose job is very physical and demanding) came home from work every day exhausted and then had to make dinner, put the kids to bed, and then reassure and comfort me for hours, as I was so anxious and depressed about the state of my health.

I felt like such a burden, and I just wanted to die. I hated feeling so dependent. I had just turned 30, and I couldn't drive, and I could barely walk because I was so weak and always sick and so afraid of getting dizzy. I also felt I was missing my kids' childhood. I couldn't play with them or take them to a park. That broke my heart so much, and the guilt just completely consumed me. I saw no way out."

Vanessa describes the first changes on an emotional level as being "very subtle and gradual; but after a few months, change in this area was very evident.

"Some of the first change I saw was an ability to think clearer. I could feel this dark cloud of gloom, despair, and depression slowly lift off me. This allowed me to think more positively and even feel happiness and hope—something I had not felt for a long time. It sounds strange, but I was so negative before that I felt like I could not even think positively if I tried, whereas with the gradual change, I actually started being happy. It was strange!"

Corresponding with the emotional changes Vanessa experienced, she reported that on a physical level she felt much stronger. She hardly had any jaw pain, her rashes were almost gone, and she experienced little dizziness. At this time, Vanessa was ready to move past the surface symptoms and issues and delve into some of the deeper issues and root causes that started in childhood.

A lot of Vanessa's anxiety developed at the age of eight when she moved from Canada to the country of her parents' birth, an

Eastern Bloc country just after the fall of Communism. In stark contrast to the comfort and safety she felt in Canada, she found herself in a different new world. The cold cement structure of the school with bars on the windows was frightening to her, the teachers were terrifying, and the culture was very confusing. She describes her teachers as "allowed to use corporal punishment on all the kids," and says teachers "often verbally taunted and poked fun at their class."

"I became petrified of the teachers and would think of ways I could avoid their fury, so I studied very, very hard. All my work had to be perfect so that they could not find any fault with it and be mad at me. I also got in trouble a few times at school for forgetting to bring certain things to school, like a button from home for sewing class. Every night as I lay in bed, I worried and made my stomach ache while rehearsing the next day at school. I thought that, surely, if I made myself sick and hurt with worry, I would remember everything I needed for school the next day; and it would motivate me to be an excellent student. I would avoid my teachers getting angry with me."

During this session, we did an Age Identity correction dealing with fears and trauma that were locked into her cellular memory from this time period. Here we identified a key maladaptive belief system:
— *If I worry enough to make myself sick, then I will be okay.*

It was a revelation to Vanessa that, even as an adult and a mother, she still worried about things to the extent that it physically hurt and made her ill because, in some way, she believed it would protect her from something worse happening.

Vanessa recalls how she felt physically different after working through this correction:

"I actually felt lighter, like I was floating on clouds, and like a super heavy weight that I didn't even know was there just took off! After that

session, I felt so much calmer and at peace. Things that overwhelmed me before seemed a lot less scary. I no longer gave myself stomach aches because of worrying about something so much. This was a huge turning point for me, and I felt I truly saw the power of Natural Bioenergetics. And it wasn't just me who saw the difference; my husband and my parents saw it too, which was so exciting."

The next phase in our work together was all around building positivity, joy, confidence, and resilience back into her life. One activity Vanessa did for homework was a visualization where she created a place of bliss. We tested the parameters together, and each day she visualized this place.

It was a place on the ocean she visited as a child with her parents. In her visualization, she saw the harbor and boats, smelled the salt in the air mixed with the smell of fish 'n' chips, felt the sun on her face, and listened to the sound of the tug boats and seagulls. While she did this, she relaxed and smiled and felt blissful. Here she experienced a sense of vitality, life, fun, and excitement.

Vanessa describes her visualization experience:

"Sharon and I created a scenario/scene in my head where I could feel blissful. It was my favorite beach. She helped me describe all the sights, sounds, smells, and details. At home, I laid down with my eyes closed and rehearsed this blissful scene in my head every day. I got into that feeling of bliss and tried to sit in it for as long as I could. Sharon also talked with me about how I could have control over negative thoughts, and she gave me some tips on how to catch those thoughts and create new pathways of positive thinking. I worked on these things diligently every day at home."

After working with Vanessa for a year, she states she cannot believe the changes that occurred in her life during that year. One of those changes is her energy level.

"The energy that I have now really changed my life for the better! Even before my breakdown, I used to have to nap when my kids did just to get *through the day because I was just so exhausted. Being so tired all the time was a huge source of frustration for me for many years, even before I had children. After a few months of seeing Sharon, I realized one day that I had no desire or need to sleep during the day. I was so overjoyed! Today I have so much more energy than I ever thought I could, allowing me to live the kind of life I want. I can meet with friends without feeling drained, I can take care of the kids all day long without passing out at 8:00 pm, and I can go for long walks too."*

She describes three other beneficial changes she noticed in that year: improved immune system, feeling stronger and improved working ability.

"After only five months of seeing Sharon, I noticed a change in my immunity. I had no colds or infections during that time. We even had some family members stay with us and later found out one had strep throat, but I didn't get it. I was really amazed!

"I also felt stronger emotionally. For instance, before, if I had a really bad day, I felt down and cried a lot. That emotion drained me for the next few days, and I had headaches from crying. I still have an emotional day here and there and cry, but I bounce back the next day.

"I even went back to work! I only work once a week, but even that was too stressful and overwhelming for me at one point in my life. Now, I thoroughly enjoy work, and I do not experience the same amount of anxiety that I used to. I notice that I can think clearer at work and adapt to new programs and changes at work a lot easier."

She also describes an "amazing yet totally unexpected transformation" that occurred regarding what she explains as her "long disordered relationship with food."

"There have been some other shifts and changes in my life that I really did not expect from Natural Bioenergetics. These are things that we didn't

specifically work on but were related to other issues. For instance, not only am I now able to eat anything that I want, but I was surprised to notice that my long-disordered relationship with food changed! At age 16, I developed anorexia; although a few years later I could eat more, I still had a very unhealthy relationship with food and with my body.

"I noticed that over the months of seeing Sharon I lost that intense desire to control my food, and my body. It was no longer always on my mind. Anyone who has a disordered relationship with food and weight knows how huge that is. I thought this was just something that I would have to live with and deal with forever as a result of having anorexia as a teenager. But my obsessive need to control is simply gone, and I feel very healthy and happy!

"I have a normal relationship with food now: I eat when I'm hungry, I can stop when I am full, and the desire to binge or stuff myself with food is simply gone. I can even eat and enjoy things that before would have caused enormous guilt and shame. Most of the time, I crave healthy meals, which I didn't think would happen if I just let go of my need to control the type of food I ate as well as the quantity. It's such an amazing feeling to actually feel in tune with my body instead of being at war with it."

A common consensus (or belief system) is that once you have an eating disorder, it is something that you must manage for the rest of your life. This is where I would like to challenge your thinking. If you think you will have to manage for the rest of your life, you are probably right. But if you open yourself up to the mindset of "it is possible to overcome this," you may end up pleasantly surprised. As Henry Ford said, "Whether you think you can, or you think you can't, you are right."

My hope is that Vanessa's story will help you to think in a new way as to what is possible, not in just the area of food but also in other areas of your life.

It was exciting working with Vanessa and seeing her literally transform before my eyes. She is not the same person today as when she came through my door a year ago. For me, as a person who delights in seeing people overcome obstacles and become well in all areas of their lives, it gives me great joy to hear her exclaim, "I finally have my life back!"

It was exciting to see Vanessa going from a place of being overwhelmed with her family responsibilities to being someone who radiates joy as she says, "I love being a Mom!"

I admire Vanessa for her openness to do the deep work, her willingness to persevere even at times when the progress seemed slow, and her overall commitment to getting well. I continue to have the privilege of working with Vanessa.

About the Author

Sharon Mathews is an Advanced Natural Bioenergetics Specialist and has been working in this field since 2013. She is passionate about empowering people to move forward in all areas of their lives. Sharon works with people who are looking to make sustainable, long-term changes and improve their overall well-being. She personalizes each session to the unique situations and needs of her clients, using techniques that help restore balance and vitality.

Born in New Zealand, Sharon now lives with her family in British Columbia, Canada.

She co-owns a Natural Health company with her husband Brian, who is President of NB Global and also an Advanced NB Specialist. They have three adult children. Their eldest, Sarah, became a NB Specialist in 2020.

Contact Sharon:
To schedule an in person or on-line appointment please email: info@bioenergeticbydesign.com.
Website: www.bioenergeticbydesign.com

Successfully Self-Employed

Eva-Maria Willner

Sarah's dream was to be her own boss. But she had no self-worth and low self-confidence, was afraid of darkness, felt drained, and her private life was too volatile.

"I felt that I could never bring my daily life in line with my dreams. I worried that I would always be a stressed mom to my son. I didn't want him to grow up with the image that women are stressed because I was." (Sarah)

Sarah was loved by her clients. She was a responsible, reliable co-worker employed in a physiotherapy clinic. Her dream was to have her own practice, be her own boss, and see private clients, which would net her more pay than working at the clinic. The main issue was that her private life was too volatile. She spent a lot of energy just keeping things together personally. There was just not enough energy, focus, or quietness to build her dream of her own clinic.

The other issue that interfered with this dream was that she kept taking "just one more" training, one after another. Deep down, she felt she was not yet good enough. She had very low self-worth and no stable self-confidence.

Sarah was 35 years old when she came for her first Natural Bioenergetics session, stating two goals: to quit smoking, and finally sort out her relationships. She was a single mom and a body worker, working with a wide variety of techniques like massage, lymphatic drainage, foot reflexology, cranio-sacral, shiatsu, and body awareness meditations.

She explains her dilemma:

"I just felt so drained. I thought to myself that I can't give massages, shiatsu and so on to people, tell them about relaxing and mindfulness when I myself am in such a mess."

Sarah heard me speak at an evening workshop for women. No women in her life were self-employed; her only role model was her male boss. In our society in Germany, it is normal that if you want to get into sports or music, you look for other athletes or musicians to learn from to get better together. In the field of business or personal growth, it is not yet a common practice. Sarah chose to book a session because she saw I was self-employed for many years.

Primarily, Sarah wanted to learn from and be coached by someone who already achieved what she wanted to achieve. Secondly, she chose me as her Natural Bioenergetics coach (known as Health Kinesiology in Germany) because I have a similar background working with yoga, dance therapy, body mindfulness, and running personal growth and meditation classes mainly for women. Her third reason was she was a single mom with a six-year old son and was at the moment entangled with a woman. She heard that I work with gay and bisexual people, and that I would not judge or be moralistic with her. She felt I was open-minded and that in the sessions she would have space to explore her options.

> *"I knew I could open up to you and face what I needed to see because I saw your work and felt you "walk your talk." You were a role model for me. You exemplified what I looked for: someone self-employed in this industry. All the other instructors and practitioners I worked with did their alternative work alongside a main job. You were the only woman I found that does this work full time. This was important to me."*

For the first year and a half, we worked on her needs as a woman and mother. We worked a lot on polarities: that she can be vulnerable and also extremely successful.

We addressed several primary issues:

1. She had so much energy and ideas and was often so bubbly; but she just uncontrollably threw her energy around so that afterwards she felt empty, tired, and stressed out. Sarah learned to work with her energy, to control it, not just give it away. We worked for two sessions on setting boundaries in an appropriate way.
2. Money was a daily struggle. The father of her son didn't reliably pay child support or alimony. She also financially supported her current girlfriend. Sarah felt that no matter how much money she earned, it was never enough. She felt responsible for everything, but she couldn't count on anyone else while others counted on her.
3. She was afraid of being alone. Sarah realized her codependency. But because she was afraid of darkness and solitude, she would rather be in a toxic relationship than have no relationship.

In the process of the sessions her private life improved. She broke up with her girlfriend and a few months later fell in love with a colleague she knew for years. He also worked in massage, so they easily bonded with each other on a private and professional level.

Sarah worked on issues with money, having needs, setting her own standards, and connecting with her values.

We did a group of Psychological Being/Not Beings; these are an energetically tense situation where clients feel "damned if you do, damned if you don't." Both being and not being the item in question creates stress for an individual:
— *Being alone / Not being alone*
— *Being intimate / Not being intimate*
— *Being together / Not being together*
— *Being a good mother / Not being a good mother*
— *Being true to myself / Not being true to myself*
— *Being successful / Not being successful.*

We worked through many emotional themes using a variety of psychological protocols. Many focused on being a woman and success:
- woman - success
- single mom - success
- wealthy - being good
- wealthy - being spiritual
- weak - successful
- vulnerable – successful.

In the sessions, I felt Sarah "cleaned out and moved on." She let go of old ideas about herself, how to behave, how to be good as a girl or a woman, how to be authentic, and how to be in our society without feeling like an outsider or a freak. She lost the constant feeling of "I have to be high energy and deliver around the clock; otherwise, I am drowning, or my lover will leave me."

Sarah describes her stress:

"I felt that I could never bring my daily life in line with my dreams. I worried that I would always be a stressed mom to my son. I didn't want him to grow up with the image that women are stressed because I was. I really hoped that I could finally address my issues. I think around age 35 a lot of people feel the need to clean up their act, or they'll just continue repeating their old patterns."

A lot of Sarah's childhood came up. The patterns from her parents were ingrained in her thinking and behavior, especially around the topic of money because her parents always needed to be very careful with it. Somewhere in her childhood, she learned that she was not allowed to say "No."

Sarah relates how she felt as she began the NB sessions:

"I felt heard and seen by you. This alone gave me a boost and the comfort and realization that I am OK. I felt that, with you, I could get through it. The most important thing was I learned to relax and give myself the time for my process. I was able to let go of the doubt that riddled me for years."

Before she came to me, Sarah already attempted on two occasions to be 100% self-employed but failed. She couldn't earn enough money on her own, so she went back to being employed somewhere else.

One of my favorite quotes that I drill into my clients and students is, "Most people overestimate what they can achieve in one year and underestimate what they can achieve in ten years."

My advice to her was, "Let's build a new beautiful house from the foundation up. You need a stable basement. You also need all your inner parts working together: your body, your emotions, and your mind."

The model of the inner person, the inner woman and the inner child, must work together and need to be heard by each other so that no one part will start sabotaging the other. This metaphor worked well for Sarah. She started to relax, being patient with herself, giving herself time to integrate, to reorganize her private life until she was ready for her third attempt at being self-employed.

Sarah recalls how her thinking about herself changed:

"I am generally a bubbly kinaesthetic person, but I never learned to reflect deeply and rethink values for myself. I never saw "me" before. I became more realistic about myself and saw my blind spots. I realized that

I am a people pleaser. But now I can be with people in a much healthier way, both privately and in a business context."

Sarah then began coming to me for business coaching, which meant our sessions focused on building her business. This time, she brought her goals: a time frame for flyers, advertisements, finding a suitable place for her practice, doing another exam as a health practitioner, and more.

In the business coaching sessions, we tested what stressed her when she started to postpone tasks or felt put off. Sarah explained how different this work was compared to everything she tried in the past.

She said that it "just felt kind of easy" and explained the work further:

"Not that it was easy, but that you could test, for example, the word "money" as my next issue, and it felt so right to look at that issue at that moment. After all the stress my parents had with money, I could see how this held me back from where I wanted to go.

As a bodyworker, I know how stress tightens the muscles and fascia. To feel that in me and watch how my body opened during and after the corrections was mind-blowing. As a bodyworker, I have the concept of stretching, massaging, warmth, water, then the muscles can let go. But to feel it so obviously just through reflecting and holding the right meridian points on the body was amazing."

In one session, Sarah said that she dreamed every night about having another baby with her new lover. She had this longing for another baby and an urge for nest building. During this session, it became clear to her that this dream was not a sign to get pregnant again; however real this longing felt, it was just a distraction to prevent her success again. She was, at that point, working through all the legal things that are normal for a business owner and employer; but she felt overwhelmed. By the end of that session, she realized that her dream was a sign to build a nest for herself. She needed to take care of herself by making home more cozy and relaxing and doing things for herself.

In Sarah's business-building sessions, we corrected Psychological Fears, Linked Opposites, and more. The key concepts she had to address for business were:
— Being a threat to others
— Being lonely when successful
— Legal stuff
— My work is worth €100 per hour
— Giving presentations
— Showing myself to the world
— Embarrassing myself
— Being a mother and being successful
— Being in a relationship and being a successful woman
— Being a magnet for clients
— Enduring successfully.

As we neared the end of our sessions around her business, I asked Sarah what she learned about herself and this kind of work. She replied, "I learned that everyone needs this work!"

Looking back, I asked Sarah to explain more about what she learned.

"If you need mentoring or coaching, see someone with NB. It makes absolute sense to first balance an issue to remove the stress and then learn/integrate it or look at it.

I needed to change deeply rooted beliefs and behavior, to renew my personal puzzle. I needed a full year before I was stable enough to say, 'I quit smoking forever.' I was in a good relationship with money; I was grounded enough to start a new relationship with a man.

In the second phase, I needed another 12 months to reach stable self-employment without worrying about: Will I have enough clients? Will they pay the price? Will they stay? What if I create another drama? Will I sabotage my success?

We worked on so many different aspects. For example, I still remember clearly when I came to the session with a bunch of documents, all the legal requirements for my business. I was already freaked out just from looking at the documents. You did a balance with me where I had to look at a document. I sweated like mad, and then I could see it gradually. Then I understood it gradually, and then I understood. I got clear. I realized I knew a lot of it and could identify what I still had to find out. I could understand it and tackle it after that session.

Maybe all this sounds childish to someone else, but I realized more and more that balancing first and then taking new information on board is a fantastic working process. I remember when my son came a few times to Eva, and she corrected his stress on the letters b and d, p and q, m and w; suddenly, it was much easier for him to read. Of course, he then had to practice; but he could do it with less resistance. His teacher in school was astonished at how quickly he improved in reading and writing. The process works on anything!

Before working with you, I used to drain all my energy and still didn't achieve what I wanted to achieve. Now I am much more relaxed, more focused. When I lose it or freak out, I am pretty quickly back in my center. I think I drive my loved ones less mad. I know I can be a drama queen, but now I can laugh about it, and it occurs much less frequently. I am definitely a happier person."

Working with Sarah was as big a growth experience for me as it was for her. My biggest realization in my work with Sarah was that meaningful homework, what we call "Life Balance" activities, is so important, as what goes on between sessions is critical to how a client progresses. Homework can be writing in a diary, having a daily affirmation, visualization, or setting rituals to stay on the path.

In everyday challenges, it is so easy to fall back into old patterns; homework keeps the client on the right track. The home environment, daily habits, and supportive relationships reinforce all the corrections conducted in NB sessions. With this support, the client can more easily flourish, integrate, flow, and blossom with new behaviors.

Through working with Sarah, my focus shifted to not only "being on the ball in the sessions" but also to test the right homework, rituals, mediation time, and other lifestyle changes, so that the deeply desired transformation can be sustained and integrated quickly.

I recently enjoyed a visit with Sarah in her own practice location, a fantastic place in the middle of town, yet very quiet. It was suitable for single sessions and for groups, meeting all her desires. She did it. She was 100 percent self-employed, in a stable growing relationship, enjoying her son, and happily running a busy practice of her own.

If you are ready to start your journey from the inside out to create the life and business you want, please contact me.

About the Author

For over 30 years, Eva-Maria Willner worked with various kinesiology directions, coaching techniques, movement, and meditation. Whether it is individual sessions, groups, team coaching or training, her focus is supporting people to be more aware of themselves, tune in to their inner guidance, and find their own path. She is convinced that everyone has a purpose and that NB provides techniques to hear "your inner call" so that you have the courage and energy to go for it. In recent years, her focus is on aging well, staying inspired, fulfilled, and healthy.

She is the Founder and leader of the Meridianum Kinesiology Institut since 1998 in Germany, an NB-teacher and teacher trainer, Transformations Kinesiology educator, Meditation teacher, Dancetherapist and Coach. She also is Co-Owner of a delightful Seminarhaus in the Black Forest (Schenkenzell, Southern Germany), where the year-round classes, workshops, and training happen.

Eva-Maria Willner
Meridianum - Institut und Schule für Kinesiologie
Reinerzaustrasse 24
D-77773 Schenkenzell
Germany
Telephone: 0049 (0)7836 - 957 9922
Fax: (0049) (0)7836 - 957 9911
Email: emw@meridianum.de
Website: www.meridianum.de
www.facebook.com/Meridianum-Institut-und-Schule-für-Kinesiologie

Animal Behavioral Issues

Cheryl Hannah

I grabbed my practitioner manual and tools and marched out to the reception area where the miscreant—a budgie—was located. I then proceeded to use Natural Bioenergetics to do corrections on him for controlling his libido. It worked instantly and permanently! The bird never rang the bell or assaulted anyone again.

My work is never boring, especially when animals are involved. Over the years, I have had the fun and privilege of working with performance horses, parrots, hamsters, komodo dragons, fish, dogs, cats, goats, sheep, and pigs, to name just a few.

One of the most memorable animals I worked with was a little male budgie named Ola. Ola was the pet of my friends, Shane and Lorin, whose story is told elsewhere in this book.

Budgies are flock birds. When there is only one budgie in a home, the owners become the "flock" for the bird, and the source of the budgie's security and happiness. Ola was used to flying free for periods of time in his home and perching on his owners' shoulders and interacting with them. However, when his flock had to go away on extended health-related trips, I became Ola's pet sitter.

One of Ola's less-desirable behaviors was acting like an uncontrollable teenage boy with one thing on his mind. This would manifest as him landing on a person's foot and pretending it was a girl budgie he wanted to make babies with. This was embarrassing for Lorin, a huge source of boisterous laughter for Shane, and not a little disconcerting for the visitor.

Another way this behavior showed up was with a perch in Ola's cage. This particular perch had a bell attached to it. Ola's habit was to land on the perch, grab one of the bars and do his thing. You would know that he was doing his thing by the rhythmic ringing that would start and increase in speed and intensity and then suddenly stop when he had "finished." Then he would fly to the opposite end of the cage and turn his back on the perch as though to say he was done with "her." This cycle would go on hour after hour.

Shane recalls:

"It drove Lorin crazy because she couldn't have him in the living room with us. It was impossible to watch TV with this racket going on in the background."

This behavior probably would have continued indefinitely if Shane and Lorin had not charged me with looking after Ola while they were on extended medical-related trips. To make things more convenient for me, I moved Ola from his home to my office, where he became a source of amusement for clients waiting to see me. He behaved for the most part; but he soon became a source of distraction while I worked with clients. I would hear the bell start to ring and go through its pattern of frenzied ringing and I would know what was going on. Very distracting and not an energy I wanted in the office!

Shane says:

"He would do this 20, 30, 40 times a day! I would laugh because I remember being a teenage boy and could totally relate."

If it had just been once or twice a day, maybe I would have left him alone. But no – this bird had no shame and no self-control. It was sometimes multiple times in an hour. So it didn't take more than a few days for me to decide I needed to do something about this.

After a client left my office, I grabbed my practitioner manual and tools and marched out to the reception area where the miscreant was located. I then proceeded to do NB corrections on him for controlling his libido. It worked instantly and permanently! After that, Ola never rang the bell or assaulted anyone again.

Ola also found it emotionally tricky when his flock was gone for long periods, even though he got plenty of attention in my office.

Shane recalls:

"We would come back from a trip and let Ola out of the cage to fly around, and he wouldn't talk to us. He would fly by us, but then he'd go sit over on the mirror and turn his back to us and refuse to interact.

Normally, he would just come over and visit and chirp and chatter. If we had been away for a few days or a month, he would ignore us for at least a couple of weeks or longer. He clearly showed his displeasure, and sometimes a month would pass before he would start talking and interacting with us again.

When we mentioned to you what was going on, you discovered that he was pissed off at us."

Budgies are highly social birds. To have his whole flock disappear was highly upsetting to this little guy. I worked up the issue and identified the psychological items that were needed. This alerted us to the fact that he was really angry and upset with his owners for abandoning him.

Shane describes the outcome of the corrections:

"You did some corrections and, while it didn't cure the problem completely, because of his social needs, he would not go to the extremes he had before of weeks or months to recover. Usually, within about an hour of our being home, he would start interacting with us. Lorin really appreciated that."

Parrots are another favorite of mine to work with. One small parrot, adopted by a friend, had a bad habit of attacking the face of anyone wearing glasses. This was pretty scary if you were wearing the glasses, as those beaks and claws can cause real damage. After a few sessions of corrections and the attacks stopped.

Another parrot was in the habit of thinking his owner was his mate. This was fine until the day she brought a boyfriend home. Then, the large grey parrot attacked the boyfriend any time he visited his girlfriend. After several sessions with me, the bird stopped attacking the boyfriend and would even let him carry him and pet him.

Behavioral issues are not the only thing that can be addressed with animals through Natural Bioenergetics. While we are not veterinarians and don't provide health care for animals, sometimes, when we work on behavioral or performance issues with animals. The NB correction work also helps animals recover from some minor illness or dysfunction they experience. It is a happy side effect of removing the stressful behavior or emotion.

About the Author

In 2002, Cheryl Hannah Nicholson was ill with a systemic yeast infection covering her entire body with an extremely itchy, raised red rash and the onset of allergies to food, animals, and more. This crisis launched her journey into the world of energy medicine.

In the summer of 2003, with a six-week-old baby in tow, Cheryl took an intensive course in Kinesionics, six days a week for the entirety of the summer. She did all her clinicals, wrote her exams, and became certified in Kinesionics. A friend insisted she needed to learn Natural Bioenergetics, so she started training in late 2010.

Now a Certified Natural Bioenergetics Specialist and teacher, one of Cheryl's chief joys, besides working with clients, is to mentor new students. NB allows her to successfully work on a wide range of conditions and imbalances with people all over the world. People easily connect with her because of her background in natural healing, herbalism, natural childbirth, and doula work.

Contact Cheryl Hannah Nicholson
Email: kinesionics@gmail.com
Cell: 250-552-3495
https://www.kinesionics.ca/

A New Lease on Life

Linda Orr Easthouse

Franky Kossy was diagnosed with two fibroids, but she had never really had a problem until the day they exploded, and she began to bleed uncontrollably.

"Before my Natural Bioenergetics sessions with Vivian, I had started isolating and became very shy about going out. I always felt very self-conscious, as I looked slightly pregnant from the fibroids. I couldn't sleep while the fibroids flared up." (Franky)

I love it when miracles happen in a concise period; it's amazing to see transformations happen fast. But it is also the reality that we work with the body—we respect the body's cycles and patterns. Sometimes it takes time, and the body may not resolve things as instantly as we would like. But, even in such cases, the body brings a degree of balance and harmony so that people can function with their ongoing issues; we address the acute symptoms, while other things seem to wait, and we let nature play its role.

I want to share the story of a woman who had a medical crisis at the beginning of her NB training. Franky is now a certified specialist and instructor and allows me to share her story here.

Content Warning: the following account contains graphic descriptions of women's issues.

Franky woke up one morning with her period, but it was not like normal! She was 44 years old and participating in her first Natural Bioenergetics class with Vivian as her instructor. She told her teacher what was going on. Vivian began a session with Franky to see what NB could do to stop the bleeding.

Franky recalls how her NB sessions started:

"I woke up one day with a period that looked like my whole body was bleeding into the toilet. I was absolutely horrified and didn't know what to do. I called the doctor, made an appointment, and ended up at a gynecologist's office, who suggested two things:

1. A hysterectomy, because in those days that was the primary option, or

2. A myomectomy, which is a procedure to take fibroids out. I was warned they often returned after surgery.

"This was back in 1997, so the techniques are a lot better these days. They had just started the new laser ablation, which I investigated, but I chickened out because I was scared of the surgery. I went to Vivian instead."

Franky's mother had had a hysterectomy when she was 44, and here was Franky, having hemorrhaging periods at the same age. It was worrisome. She did not want to follow in her mother's footsteps and have a hysterectomy, and she was terrified of having surgery.

Two weeks earlier, she was diagnosed with two fibroids, but she had never really had a problem until the day they exploded, and she began to bleed uncontrollably. Her weight was yo-yoing up and down, and she was cramping more than usual. Once she got the diagnosis, Franky calculated she probably had the fibroids for a year. The doctor checked for ovarian cancer, but the test came back negative; it was just fibroids.

She began taking homeopathic remedies to reduce the bleeding. Franky started to working with Vivian every month:

"I knew I did not want an operation; I wasn't going to try something that was still very experimental. Everybody said, "Oh, they're going to shrink when you go through menopause." But I was at least six years away from that point in my life, so NB ended up being my only option. I just fell in love with the work."

The first session addressed the "Energy of two fibroids." It included primarily psychological issues around inferiority and security. By the second appointment, the bleeding was a little reduced. Two months later, Franky had a second ultrasound. Surprisingly, it showed three fibroids instead of two. The original one was larger but softer; something was changing as the bleeding was reducing slowly.

Discouraged, Franky agreed to the embolization (scraping off the fibroids). She did all the prep work for the procedure and was awaiting surgery when the time for her next NB appointment came.

This session included a group of workaround self-sabotage:
— *Sabotaging my energy body-mind-spirit*
— *Sabotaging my life*
— *Sabotaging my fibroids*
— *Sabotaging my love life.*

They also did some Membrane Configurations. This protocol allows the cells to take nutrients in and let waste products out:
— *Experiencing health*
— *Knowing I can be healthy*
— *Healthy all the time.*

This was followed by a psychological group called Being/Not Being. This is about feeling damned if you do and damned if you don't—you feel stressed no matter what you do.
— Being normal
— Not being normal
— Being satisfied
— Not being satisfied.

The session ended with corrections around "Life is one big happy event."

Franky returned a month later but had been sick throughout most of this time. She again had a lot of pain and heavy bleeding and had suffered two weeks of sinusitis. The fibroids caused her uterus to be swollen and uncomfortable. She could not sleep on her stomach. However, by the time Franky's surgery date arrived, the abnormal bleeding stopped, so she was able to cancel the surgery. What a relief!

Vivian continued to work with Franky. Two months later, the level of menstrual bleeding was average, even though the fibroids were still present and bulging. This session was fascinating because it used eight of the "cosbat" energy tools in pairs down the front of the torso as part of a process for sedating and lowering the energy levels. At the same time, they did corrections around hormones, allergies, and chemicals. This was followed by some work-around words that triggered Franky's fight-or-flight response.

Franky recalls the change in her life:

"When the bleeding sort of petered out, it gave me a whole new lease on life. Previously, I ran from one pharmacy to the next, terrified that I would run out of what I needed—a lot of tampons and pads because I was bleeding so heavily. It really knocked my confidence a lot. I was in business at the time and having meetings with people. I was always worried that something was going to show. The fact that NB worked gave me a lot more confidence to bounce back to my former self."

It took five treatments over a few months for the bleeding to get back to normal levels. The following month, Franky had another session. She came in angry that "nothing was working." She was angry at her body—even though the bleeding was now normal, the fibroids were still there. This session brought up some of the core underlying themes and assumptions that affected her:

— *Parents are a blessing in my life*
— *Women are better friends.*

A month later, she explored those assumptions through a journaling exercise. Franky had to write whatever came to mind on the assigned topics. It was the same set of questions, three times a week, for a month. The topics to address were:

1. *If I let myself feel again, how will I react?*
2. *If I understand what happens to me, how can I do energy work?*
3. *When I do what I think I want to do, why do I feel dissatisfied?*

Psychological shifts were happening. Franky was now OK with the process, even though it was somewhat slow. That session also included a lot of Spin corrections, which change the energy of tissues and restore healthy magnetic spin to the cells.

Two months later, the issues turned to the second big theme: knowing when to let go. This brought up the following psychological corrections:

— *Feeling looked after*
— *Me knowing how I feel*
— *Feeling annoyed*
— *I feel left alone.*

Linked Opposites is a correction where opposite thoughts get frozen together and sabotage the processing of positive emotions:

— *Forgiving and alone*
— *Focused and trapped*

— *Resourceful and bewildered*
— *Sexy and ashamed.*

Vivian helped Franky complete additional Psychological Fear work around the emotions of knowing when to let go:
— *Fear of being alone*
— *Fear that I am not good enough*
— *Fear that I can't be good*
— *Fear that I feel OK when I am alone*
— *Fear of knowing when to let go.*

Finally, another Being/Not Being correction:
— *Being ashamed*
— *Not being ashamed*
— *Being not ashamed.*

Franky's final session with Vivian ended with two corrections that drew the line under this whole body of work around fibroids, allowing Franky to focus on other aspects of life. She worked through:
— *How can I become free of all the old patterns and behaviors?*
— *How can I become free of my past?*

Looking back from the other side of menopause, with the fibroids gone, Franky shared her reflections with me:

"As much as I believed that it was going work, the fact that NB really did help surprised me. Eventually, the fibroids shrank, and then menopause got rid of them altogether. It gave me a sort of new lease on life. A lot of the things that came out in those sessions emotionally were spot on. It was good. Like a miracle."

Franky recognizes how much her emotional and mental processes fed into the fibroids. Yet, doing this work allowed her to find a fulfilling relationship, change with grace into a career she loves, and rebuild her view and respect of herself. What incredible side effects of working on fibroids!

If you have some work to do, please contact Franky or any of the specialists who shared stories in this book. We would be glad to work with you to see what you want to heal. There is always a way.

About the Author

Linda Orr Easthouse is a stress management coach, energy medicine professional, radionics master, and best-selling author. With more than 15 years experience as a Natural Bioenergetics Specialist, she helps people change their patterns so that they can become whatever they want to be. Using therapies that restore the body, mind, and spirit, she assists people to take control of their stresses, establish healthy patterns, and gain control over their success and future. Many athletes and business owners seek her assistance to optimize their performance and outcomes.

Linda has a MA and many years of apprenticeship in the healing arts. She is the Director of the Natural Bioenergetics Institute. Her book, Pushing the Reset Button: The busy professional's guide to a healthy lifestyle, made the Amazon best-seller list and has been sold worldwide.

Book a private session with Linda.
www.lindaeasthouse.com
Take a class with Linda.
www.naturalbioenergetics.ca
FB: Yourpowerfullife
Instagram: @lindaeasthouse
Email: Linda@Naturalbioenergetics.ca

A Natural Bioenergetics Primer™

Introduction to Natural BioEnergetics™

Did you know that our bodies have an innate ability to sustain health and balance? However, sometimes our bodies need a little help to activate these natural abilities, and that's where Natural BioEnergetics™ Professionals come in. NB Professionals are trained to help our bodies heal themselves by balancing your whole energy system and, in doing so, facilitate a self-healing process.

Natural BioEnergetics™ Professionals use gentle muscle testing, combined with verbal questioning to communicate directly with your body's unique energy system. This technique involves applying light pressure to a muscle (commonly your arm) and monitoring how it responds.

- If the muscle holds steady, the system is responding with a 'yes.'
- If the muscle is weakened (unlocks), the answer to the muscle response question is 'no.'

In this way, the NB Professional is able to communicate directly with your innate self. Your body is able to respond quickly and accurately to the Natural Bioenergetic procedures.

This can be much more helpful than having to "guess" or "figure it out," order elaborate medical testing, or just wait to see if the problem goes away on its own.

Muscle Monitoring Works

Muscle monitoring works, *if you do it correctly*, for two reasons:
- Your body uses an **Autonomic Control System (ACS)** to unconsciously control all body functions needed to keep us alive and well. There are 50 trillion cells this system controls. It knows everything that is happening in your body. But this information is all unconscious to us. The

brilliant part is your body will respond to yes or no questions in this system with a simple muscle response.
- It works because of what quantum physics calls **Quantum Entanglement**. At the unconscious level, you know everything I know, and I know everything you or your body knows. The connection established between the NB professional and you, the client, means together, you can find a way to have a healthier mind, body, and soul.

Bioenergetics Wellness

In the natural health field, the term **Bioenergetics Wellness** is used to indicate the many systems which have sprung from Applied Kinesiology and historically were called Specialized Kinesiology. Here, muscles become monitors of stress and imbalance within the body. Thus, the concept of "muscle testing" is more accurately called **muscle monitoring** and becomes a very effective and versatile tool for detecting and correcting various imbalances in the body, which may relate to stress, nutrition, learning problems, injuries, and trauma.

A Holistic Approach

Natural Bioenergetics (*formerly called Health Kinesiology*) is a holistic approach to personal development, health, and well-being. It uses "muscle monitoring" to access information from the subconscious mind to be able to direct the practitioner on how to bring about health and well-being.

Natural Bioenergetics explores the science of mind-body-environment relationships. It is based on an interdisciplinary science concerned with the interactions of matter, energy, and consciousness. It integrates the wisdom of traditional eastern medicine and the more recent western understanding of the body, providing the best of both approaches.

Natural Bioenergetics involves studying, researching, and

applying the biophysics and technology of the mind, brain, spirit, consciousness, to the underlying forces of life and nature expressed in the physical realm.

Natural Bioenergetics triggers repair based on the principles of Traditional Chinese Medicine (TCM), which asserts that our well-being depends on the balanced flow of energy around our systems. By re-balancing the energy, the energy then provides improved information to the body about how to structure itself and function, which triggers self-healing.

Natural Bioenergetics uses the concept of BALANCE to indicate that the entire electromagnetic field of the person (biofield) is in homeostasis and able to communicate with all the major feedback systems in the body. Balance ensures that the flow of light and electrons to nerve pulses and other feedback systems can make complete circuits and the system is not in a fight or flight stress response.

Many factors can upset the flow around our system of energetic information governing structure and function (the Autonomic Control System of western medicine) and put it out of balance, including the following:

- Environmental toxins, allergens, microorganisms, electromagnetic fields, and other frequencies
- Psychological stresses like worries, fears, or limiting assumptions we may have about ourselves

These factors may block the flow of information around our bodies and cause the affected parts to forget how to grow and work correctly.

Using the techniques in NB, the NB Professional is able to identify the factors causing the blockages and restore healthy structure and function.

Our bodies are doing their best to communicate with us...
- that twinge of pain
- the pang of indigestion
- the headache
- the backache

- the depression
- the general feeling of being out of sorts

All of these are signals from the body that we need to make positive changes in our lives.

The NB Professional works directly with the client to listen carefully to the symptoms and address the real root issues.

ASSESSMENT

The NB Professional uses gentle muscle monitoring to open a communication channel with your body to assess the situation.

CORRECTIONS

Using the Natural Bioenergetics' uniquely designed system of protocols, the body can access the existing energy library and select corrections via muscle monitoring, which will re-balance and restore correct structure and function. Corrections often come up around a theme, or several different corrections can be related to the same topic. We call that a GROUP of corrections. An individual correction is an ITEM. There will often be several ITEMS in a GROUP working on the same trauma or stress to balance all aspects of it.

Corrections will be categorized according to wherein the person's energy system they are working. So thoughts, beliefs, fears, worries, and other emotional topics that create psychological stress are referred to as PSYCHOLOGICALS.

ADJUNCTIVES are routines worked out to be done at home to support the work done in the session. They help create the environment and support for the body to process the work smoothly.

The anatomy of a CORRECTION consists of a number of key elements. Finding the appropriate stress in the body/mind/soul (the biofield). Identifying the frequency(s) needed to release the stress from the Biofield. Provide the body with the required transformational energy through the activation of acupressure points or utilization of specialized tools (like programmed gemstones), which provide the body the energy to correct the imbalance related to the stress. The procedure is held until the person can face that stressful thought or environment without going into a fight or flight response over it. In short, re-tuning the Human Biofield.

The POINTS we use are the acupuncture points, the same as used in traditional Chinese acupuncture. However, we do not use needles. Rather we hold the points lightly through the client's clothing with fingertips, magnets, or programmed quartz and other crystals.

TRIGGERS SELF HEALING

The body then responds to the renewed flow of enlivening information and repairs itself.

Natural Bioenergetics' balancing methods include the use of magnets, flower essences, aromatherapy oils, self-touch, and body positions, and acupoints and thoughts that mirror mental and emotional stresses. These are used to take power out of thoughts and memories around the traumas and beliefs at the heart of the client's mental, emotional and physical stresses.

During a typical session...

Natural Bioenergetics sessions are both deeply healing and deeply relaxing. A typical session can last 60 – 90 minutes with you lying down on a therapy couch fully clothed. If lying down is physically uncomfortable, you can sit up for the session.

As you read this, your body is hard at work, breathing, excreting toxins, balancing hormones, assimilating nutrients, and performing countless other vital functions to keep you in balance and health. **Sometimes that healthy balance is disturbed**, for example, by physical trauma, surgery, stress, toxins, electronic fields, shock, allergens, emotional or psychological stress, negative thinking, or even just long-term unhappiness. Using muscle monitoring, your NB Professional accesses your body's unique inner wisdom to find out exactly what you need to regain and maintain balance and feel truly healthy, both inside and out.

You may only need a single appointment, but more generally, people need a series of appointments. **Some clients recognize that Natural Bioenergetics™ can be used in a preventive manner rather than just dealing with problems when they arise.** These clients will continue to have sessions in order to maintain their health and well-being.

Following a session, you may...

As part of a Natural Bioenergetics™ session, your system may define essential lifestyle changes for itself as part of its recovery program, including things like:
- changing your diet or adding nutritional supplements
- using flower essences or homeopathic remedies
- initiating exercising programs
- making time for self-care, relaxing and fun

No two sessions are ever alike, even for people with apparently identical symptoms.

Most people find a Natural Bioenergetics™ session very relaxing. Some people feel pleasantly lighter and 'clearer' afterward. Some people may experience temporary feelings of tiredness and sleepiness or other slight symptoms. This is because sessions are powerful and deep-reaching and can bring about major energy changes. This is actually a good sign indicating that a healing process has already begun.

It's a good idea to drink plenty of water following a session and rest or sleep if you need to.

Who benefits?

Everyone can benefit from Natural Bioenergetics: babies, the elderly, athletes, performers, the fit, the injured, the unwell, pets...

Life can be challenging, and it is not always easy to change the things you want to change—whether that is your health, your job, your relationship, or all of these and more. Sometimes we just don't know where to start and how to keep ourselves motivated.

When our bodies start to exhibit physical symptoms, they are trying to tell us something important, and this can be difficult to interpret by ourselves. NB Professionals are able to find out why your physical, emotional, chemical, and nutritional systems have fallen out of balance and how to go about changing them for the better. This can be especially helpful for those who cannot communicate for themselves, like babies, pets, etc.

In a world where we are bombarded by information from other people, **Natural Bioenergetics lets you get information from you.** You might be surprised at how accurate NB can be.

Natural Bioenergetics can help to:

- Increase energy and vitality
- Prevent illness
- Boost your healing mechanisms and immunity
- Release negative thinking or behavior patterns
- Overcome fears and worries
- Sharpen mental focus
- Manage sports performance
- Improve relationships at home or work
- Develop your abilities
- and more!

Illness does not arrive suddenly, although it may seem to do so. Instead, it is usually the result of a build-up of stress–physical, mental, or emotional—leading to imbalances in the body/mind system, which ultimately leads to physical symptoms.

Our body has an innate ability to heal itself and does this quite naturally on a daily basis. Sometimes our system needs a bit of help, either medical or complementary or often, a combination of both. Natural BioEnergetics assists in balancing all aspects of ourselves, which returns the body to an optimum state for self-healing.

The healing effects can continue for days, weeks, and even months following a Natural BioEnergetics session. The effects of sessions are cumulative. It is possible to see a benefit from the first session, or it may take longer for the cumulative effect to be clearly noticeable to you. How long improvement takes will depend on the individual and their ability to re-balance and heal. Each client responds as well as their body and energy system is able. **Generally, the rate of improvement depends on** how long you have had the concern, how deeply rooted it is, your ability/willingness to make and sustain suggested lifestyle changes, and how good your energy levels are.

Only your body has the ability to heal itself. Regardless of where you get help and support from to find emotional, mental, and physical balance, it is just that—help. You ultimately have the responsibility for your own health.

There is a difference between being healthy and not feeling ill. If you strive to be healthy, Natural Bioenergetics will be of invaluable assistance.

Acknowledgments

This book is an essential project on many levels. It would not have happened without a team of people who contributed various aspects because they believe in its importance.

We first want to thank the Natural Bioenergetics Specialists and Instructors around the world who shared these stories of hope from their clients or from their own experiences.

We especially owe a great debt of gratitude to Lily Ayre, one of our UK Specialists who has a background as a professional editor. She took the finished drafts that each client/specialist team prepared and turned them into beautiful stories. Without her wisdom and skill, we could not have pulled this project together.

We are also deeply grateful to Divya Parekh, for her team editors who gave our stories reader perspective and her team's technical work, for her guidance in the fundraising aspects of this project, and her encouragement and flexibility in getting this done during times of COVID-19 lockdowns and disruption.

Shine Sponsors

ZACCONI WEALTH MANAGEMENT

WEALTH ADVISOR AND CERTIFIED FINANCIAL PLANNER

We are a full function Wealth Advisor service looking after all your planning needs from Retirement, Tax, Education, Estate, Credit, Life and Disability Insurance.
Visit https://www.raymondjames.ca/josephzacconi/
For a Complimentary Review of your portfolio and goals

SHINE SPONSOR

VIVIAN KLEIN

NATURAL BIOENERGETICS SPECIALIST

From the worlds of both art and business, Vivian started her NB career 30 years ago and has been a Natural Bioenergetics™ Specialist (previously HK - Health Kinesiology™) since 1991, having completed her extensive training in England (a rigorous training that included studies in Anatomy and Physiology, Counseling Skills, Nutrition and Practice Management/Business skills).
Website: viviklein.com

SHINE SPONSOR

Sublime

RECLAIM YOUR LIFE MASTERY COACHING **WITH LINDA EASTHOUSE**

Reclaim Your Life Mastery Coaching is a ground-breaking six-month group program that supports women in transforming the mind and emotions so you can maximize results in your life. We serve women who have raised their kids, worked 20+ years and now are wondering is this all there is? Is it too late for me? Where did I lose myself along the way? Regain your zest for life, rediscover your own desires and create a life that revitalizes you and your relationships.

WOMEN WHO WORK WITH ME GAIN THE STRENGTH,

wisdom and structure to let go of the emptiness, refill, and restore your dreams. Experience deep satisfaction in your life. You receive empowering mentorship from expert coaches and trainers in the field of holistic health, transformation and personal development... and access to the Natural Bioenergetics team to support you through growing pains and breakthroughs.

LINDA EASTHOUSE SUBLIME SPONSOR

This is an intense work-on-yourself program that changes you from the inside out. It is time to re-invent yourself! We help you uncover the roots of unhappiness or frustration. Symptoms will continue to show up over and over until you begin to heal the core cause of the issue. Understanding the ROOT of your overwhelming stress, poor health, or frustrating relationships, allows you to shift the entire direction of your life and call in exactly what you truly desire – and show up as the woman you want to be.

We've designed this workshop because women face the same issues repeatedly. We want to share our experiences so you can take the wins and avoid some of the losses.

Visit the Links Below!

- https://naturalbioenergetics.ca/programs/free-masterclass-thriving-chaos/
- https://www.facebook.com/groups/reclaimyourlifegroup
- https://naturalbioenergetics.ca/programs/reclaim-your-life-mastery-coaching/

Sponsor

Sublime

BIOENERGETIC BY DESIGN

At Bioenergetic by Design, we believe the body has the innate ability to restore itself to optimal health. Health is not measured only in the physical, but encompasses the whole person: body, mind and spirit. Health means so much more than just being free from pain and disease. Health is a vibrant, resilient energy that enables us to live life well.

OUR ROLE AT BIOENERGETIC BY DESIGN

is to facilitate and encourage this process and support you on your journey to full vibrant health. Rather than just following a standard protocol or doing what works for other people, we focus on what is right for you. By employing a combination of advanced techniques and modern technologies, we create a personalized healing plan designed to help you achieve your goals and bring your body into harmony and balance.

BRIAN MATHEWS — SUBLIME SPONSOR

As you gain greater awareness of your body's response to negative stimulus (emotions, fears, trauma, negative thoughts and beliefs, etc.) these stressors are released and your body is then able to heal. This allows you to gain back control of your health, achieve your goals and be the person you want to be, with the strength to do the things you love.

Bioenergetic by Design is a company focused on holistic health & wellness. Our mission is to empower our clients to seek a balanced, sustainable, and natural approach to health.

778-344-3143
www.bioenergeticbydesign.com

Bioenergetic by Design
HEALTH & WELLNESS

Sponsor